How To Shoot Weddings

By Michael K. Arin

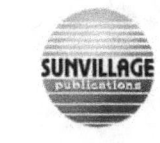

SUNVILLAGE
publications

www.sunvillagepublications.com

How To Shoot Weddings
By Michael K. Arin

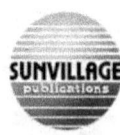

SUNVILLAGE
publications

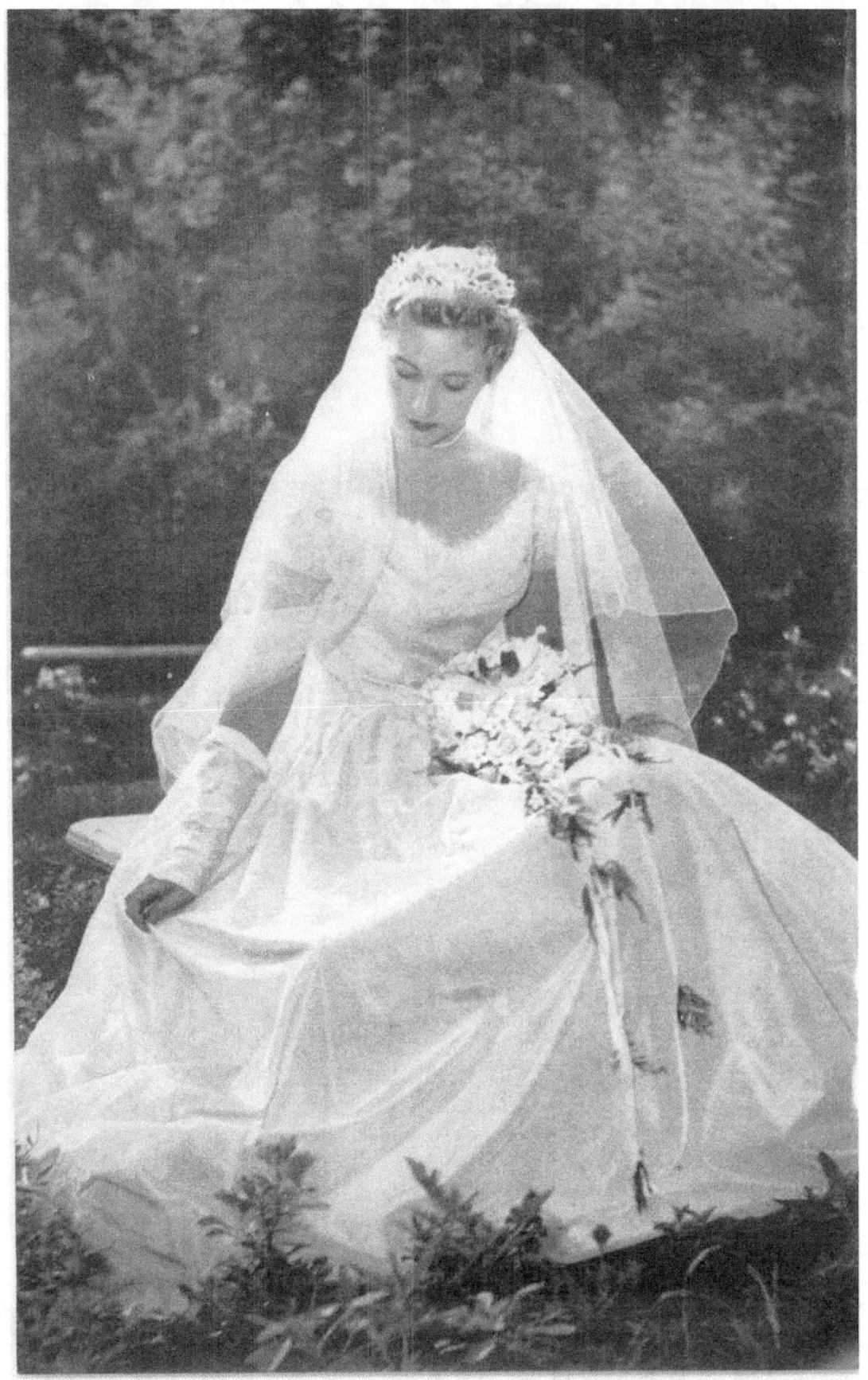

Contents

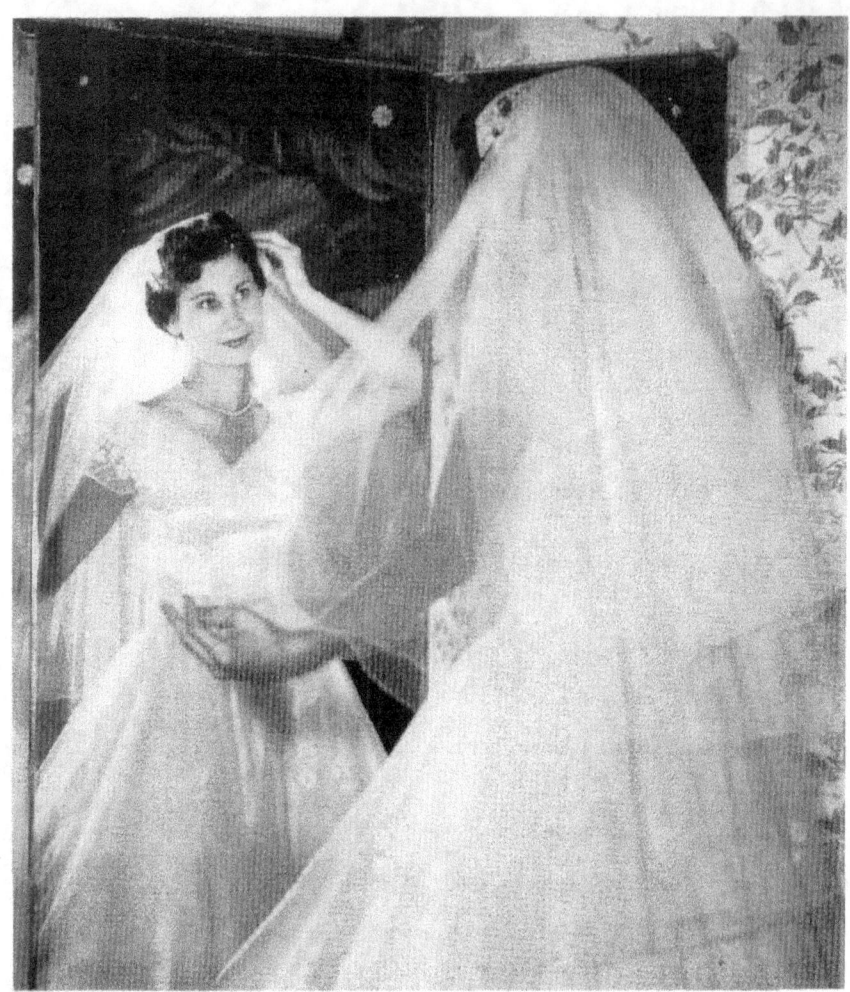

2. *This is a popular pose in the series at home before the ceremony. Stand about five feet behind the bride, move to one side until she is centered in mirror as seen through your viewfinder. Focus on the mirror image; check your camera footage scale and use this distance for figuring flash exposure. Depth of field must be sufficient to include both bride and mirror image. If bedroom ceiling is light and of normal height and if you use a No. 5 flashbulb or a 100-watt electronic flash, try "partial bounce:" Tilt reflector so some direct light strikes subject's face and the rest is reflected from ceiling. Open up two f/stops more than you would for straight flash. Watch the mirror image carefully for reflections of open closet doors, coat hangers or other unwanted details. If you cannot see your own flashgun in the mirror you will not get a glare of reflected light. The bride should have a serious expression rather than a smile for best results. (Busch Pressman; Tri-X; 60 w/s electronic flash, 1/200, f/10 second.)*

1

Introduction

CANDIDS HAVE SWEPT THE COUNTRY. According to the latest statistics, at least 1,500,000 weddings were performed in each year for the past ten years— or one wedding for every hundred people. A conservative figure of one hundred dollars for the average candid wedding order adds up to a multi-million dollar industry. And in my experience, it is rare nowadays, to find a bride without a wedding album or 3D pictures.

What kind of pictures are in demand? Styles have changed. Gone is the day of studio formals. The swing has turned to action-stopping photos. Man's ability to harness the intensity of sunlight in a little bulb of glass and to release at will this flash of brilliance, makes possible the capture of fleeting, priceless moments of the wedding day.

With this change came a new problem. In the old "studio formals" one photographer could shoot a bridal party every half hour. In "candid wedding" photography the photographer must remain for the duration of each wedding-following along from the bride's house to the church, and into the reception. It is understandable that a studio could not keep men who were needed only on Saturday and Sunday on its permanent staff. The practice was, and still is, to hire a free-lance photographer for each wedding as it is booked.

This situation did not come about abruptly. If it had, it could have played havoc with all studios, for few photographers knew much about flash. But several factors played an important part in making the transition from studio formals to candid weddings a smooth one. The public did not go out for candid wedding photography all at once. Most who ordered this type of coverage also requested studio formals as insurance, for candid results were unpredictable. A candid wedding around 1944 or 1945 was often an amateurish operation— 15 to 20 shots were considered enough. At best, the work was fair, and nobody knew the difference.

The creation of the candid wedding photographer really started about 1944. Then the G.I. Bill of Rights made possible first the education, then the availability of thousands of photographers who, though inexperienced, knew the rudiments of flash. They in turn, along with press photographers, stimulated the interest of countless amateurs in the use of the 4x5 press camera, flash and candid weddings.

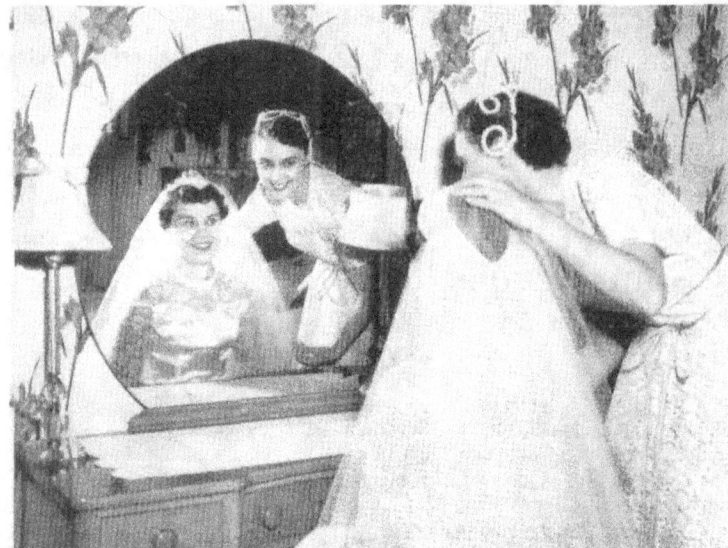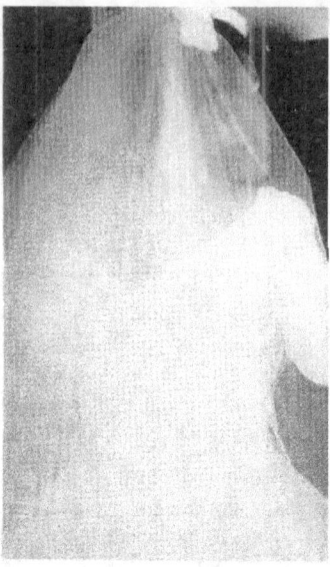

3. Bride and maid of honor together before mirror: keep heads close together and be sure that both are shown. If the bride's hands show, have her hold a comb, brush, perfume bottle, etc.—a hand mirror may cast a had reflection. A smile is more appropriate here than when the bride is photographed alone. This shot may also be made with the bride's mother or sister in attendance. (Busch Pressman; Tri-X; 80 w/s electronic flash, 1/200, f/13; film developed in DK-50.) 4. This is another version of the bride alone before the mirror, this

The Present Set-up

Today the supply of photographers meets the demands—but only in quantity, not in quality. Because standards in the candid wedding field are lower than any vocation I can think of in which people are paid for their services, there's always room for a good newcomer. Results now run the gamut from the occasional good to the more common fair or bad. A studio's reputation is in the hands of the candid men shooting its weddings. Most studios with fine portrait records have suffered, for their reputation is only as good as their least competent photographer and the negatives he exposes. Within a few years another important development came about. Wedding photography was steadily taken away from the studio by the very men it hired. Without this revenue thousands of general photography studios folded. Most were post-war ventures.

This development was a natural. Today's candid wedding photographer needs no studio. The accepted way now is to shoot "formals" (bride, bride and groom, and bridal party) with flash in the living room, church or reception hall and in warmer weather in front of the church or at the park against a background of foliage and sky. All that is needed is a few hundred dollars worth of equipment, a darkroom in an attic, basement or bathroom and the photographer is in business. Weddings occur almost exclusively on Saturdays and Sundays—the average man's day off. The candid photographer can have his regular job (usually not photography) and generously supplement his income

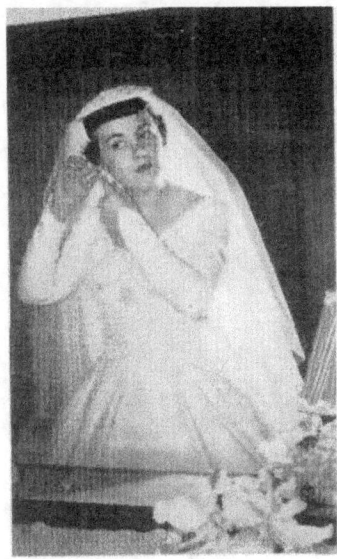
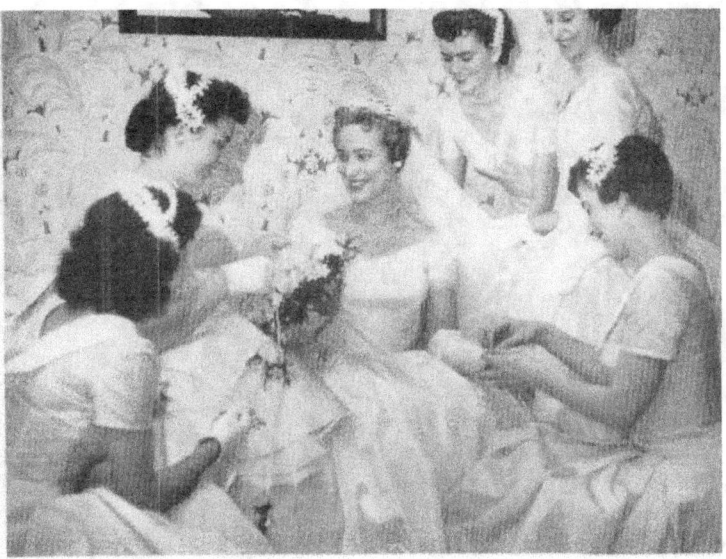

time made with the partial-bounce technique. (Konica III; Plus-X; No. 5 flash-bulb; 1/200, f/11; film developed in Microdol.) 5. Before departing for church, the bride surrounded by her attendants makes a lovely subject. The individuals are usually youthful and the realistic effect of partial-bounce flash adds naturalness to the shot. Try for a carefully-posed hut apparently in-formal grouping such as the one shown here. (Rolleifex; Tri-X; 60 w/s electronic flash, partial bounce, 1/250, f/4; developed in Microdol.)

with candids. But having this as a supplement and not the main source of in-come is, I believe, the important reason for his complacent attitude and for the almost complete lack of the one ingredient indispensable to success in any business—*competition*. Then, too, the stimulus of information or literature on the shooting of candids is conspicuously absent.

What Is Candid Wedding Coverage?

Today, covering a candid wedding has developed into a full day's project, and fifty or more photos are made. The continuity of the candid has become standardized by the public's preference for certain poses and all photographers take very much the same kind of shots. However, each photo can reflect the imagination and originality of the individual photographer. This originality, coupled with clean processing and printing, will pay big dividends in personal satisfaction as well as in dollars and cents.

The candid wedding photographer's function is an important one. To him is entrusted the recording of the wedding day—an indelible recording—never to be retaken. It can relive pleasant memories for the couple and their families, or by inferior workmanship, spoil them irreparably!

Simply producing a photographic record of the wedding day is not enough. Aside from technical excellence the photographs should contain the elements needed to sustain the "reader's" interest.

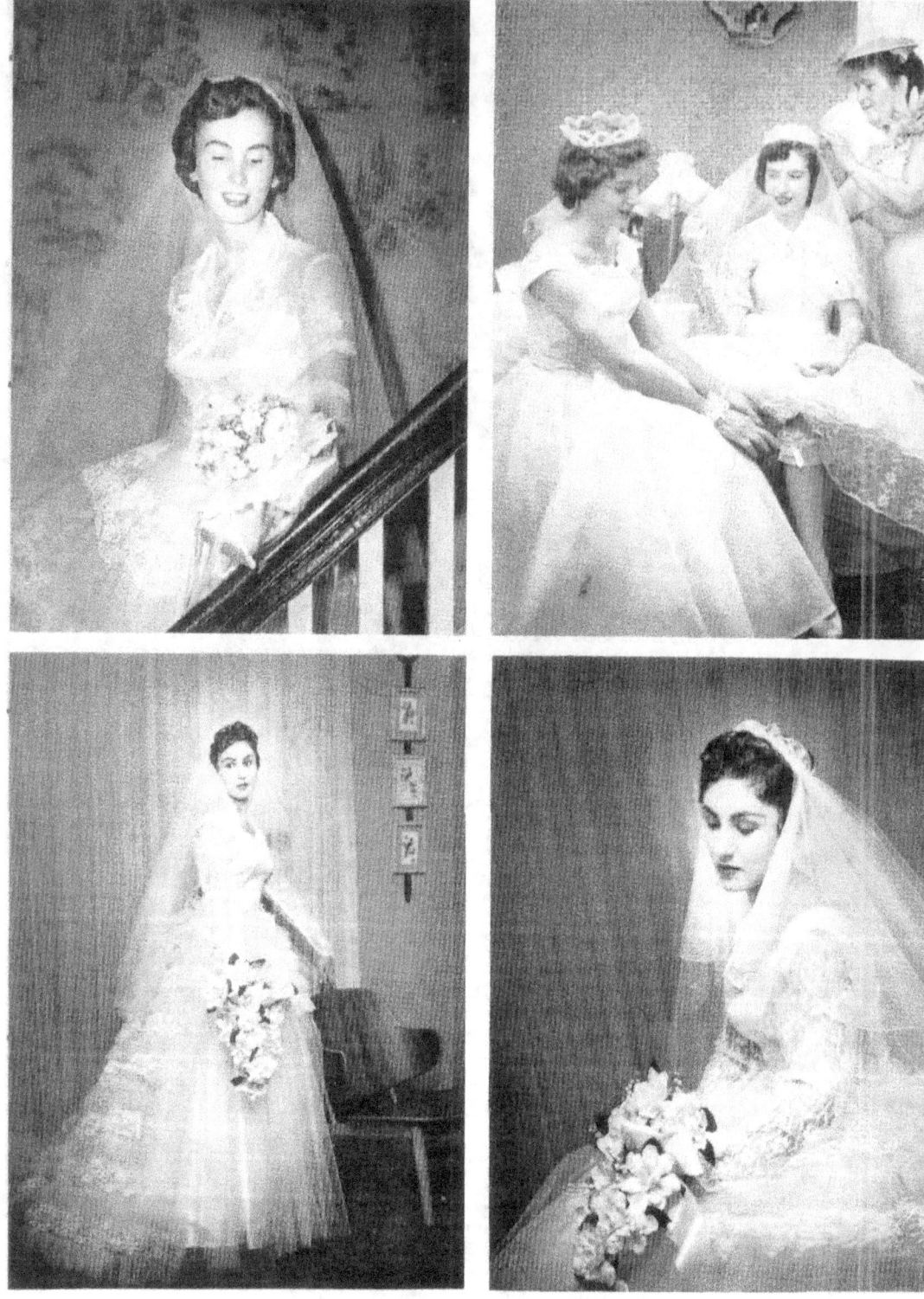

6. The bride descending the stairs is posed at the bottom to avoid the distortion which would occur if you shoot up at her from below. This gives a charming three-quarter length portrait. The wallpaper in the background was burned in to subdue the distracting pattern and prevent a conflict with the real center of interest. Sometimes there arc murals or natural backgrounds which add to the bridal mood. When you can separate bride and background, shoot with a large lens opening to throw it out of focus. (Butch Pressman; Tri-X; 80 w/s electronic flash unit, 1/200, f/16; DK-50.) 7. The bride putting on her garter is a shot best made in the bedroom. The hem of the gown should be no higher than the knee to keep this picture from becoming indelicate. (Rolleiflex Tri-X; 60 w/s electronic flash unit, partial bounce, 1/250, f/5.6; Microdol.) 8, 9. The "following photographer" is expected to take a half-dozen formal shots in addition to candid coverage during the hurried and sometimes harried preparations of the family getting ready to go to the church. There is no time for multiple lighting; all his effects must be obtained with one light. Modeling can be improved by raising the gun or by using a bare bulb or bounced flash, but the best results come from "partial bounce" techniques—some of the light strikes the bride's face directly and the rest is reflected from the walls and ceiling. (With a white ceiling, opening up two f/stops more than for straight flash will give proper negative density.) This partial bounce effect should not he used with color, however, because of the danger of introducing color casts from surrounding surfaces. To avoid distortion in the camera, shoot full-length portraits from a squatting position with the lens at about waist level. For three-quarter standing or sitting portraits, raise the lens to about the shoulder level of the subject. (Picture 8: Rolleiflex; Tri-X; 60 w/s electronic flash unit, partial bounce, 1/250, f/4; developed in Microdol. Picture 9: Rolleiflex; Tri-X; 60 w/s electronic flash unit, partial bounce, 1/250, f/5.6; film developed in Microdol.)

Available light, control of depth of field or focus, suggestion of motion through blur and even obvious grain are a few of the adjectives and adverbs of the photographic language waiting to be used by the candid wedding photographer. He has the means to inject into the prosaic, the sustained interest of the short story or perhaps even the imagery of a poem. On the other hand there are the candid wedding photographers who have little or no interest in their work other than as a way to "an extra buck." They are coasting along on last year's knowledge. For them, understandably, photography is work!

About the Word "Candid"

The expression "candid pictures" may have had its origin in the newspaper and magazine fields. It implies the taking of unposed, on the spot photos with a portable camera. Magazines such as *Look* and *Life* depend almost entirely on the candid picture, and to a lesser degree the same applies to newspapers. To them, in most instances, the picture story is all important, technical excellence secondary, and flattery inconsequential.

In candid wedding photography the exact opposite holds true; flattery is all and flattery will get you everywhere. The success of your venture depends upon the number of pictures purchased. A couple will not select a picture of themselves, regardless of its importance to the sequence of the wedding story, if they do not like the way they look. For the experienced candid wedding photographer there is no element of surprise. He is aware of every picture in the series and its problems. Consequently, there is no excuse for lack of technical competence. Throughout the entire wedding there are only five or six shots that are truly "candid." These are taken during the ceremony at the altar. Even in shots where action is taking place, such as coming down the aisle, the bridal couple can see the photographer ready to take their picture. So, the connotation of the word "candid" with wedding pictures is not so much the capturing of expressions as the stopping of action with a fast lens or flash. The public is constantly bombarded by the finest photography in the world used to sell nationally advertised products. However, people do not expect this excellence in their personal portraits or wedding photos. To them this type of photography is as remote as Hollywood or the glamorous models who smile at them from the pages of magazines; it comes as a pleasant surprise when their pictures have some of the clarity and sparkle found only in truly professional work.

How *This Book Will Help* You

The primary purpose of this book is to provide the necessary know-how for shooting a "professional" candid wedding. It will be an invaluable guide to the photographer contemplating candid for profit, and equally invaluable to the one now shooting professionally who is interested in smoothing out possible rough edges.

A second, though not secondary, purpose is my desire to elevate the standards of our field and by so doing to place it on a par, in the mind of the public, with the established portrait studios and their consistently acceptable photographic results.

2

The Candid Wedding

/~\NE THOUSAND QUESTIONS in the form of one thousand mental gremlins ^ plague the tyro photographer on his first wedding job. How do you expose a mirror shot? How do you group a bridal party? How do you . . . . but as I said, there are a thousand questions! And the only oracle that can bring forth the answers is: Experience. This is your gremlin-chaser. And it is this book's intention to make the pathway to experience a shorter and smoother one.

The outline that follows is broken down into the general classifications of House, Church, Formals, Reception and Other Shots. It includes all the more popular shots taken during the wedding day. Each shot, in turn, is again broken down to answer the How, When, Why and Where. And before that gremlin pulls your f/stop from f/8 to 22, these are the facts that will stop him cold.

1. AT THE BRIDE'S HOUSE

The day has arrived and the fatal hour is approaching. So let's take a final check. The time: 2:00 P.M. Wedding ceremony: 4:00 P.M. Trip to bride's house: 20 minutes. Trip from bride's house to church: 10 minutes. We should be at the bride's house: 3:00 P.M. (about fifty minutes before the bride leaves for church). If this were a Jewish wedding, where the reception and ceremony are held at one establishment, the bride would arrive about one hour before the ceremony, and so would we.

Now a final check. No flat tires? Cameras loaded? Extra film? Speedlight charged and working? Flashbulbs and gun in case of speedlight trouble?

The day is cold, so about five minutes before leaving, we'll start the motor and heater to warm the car. A cold camera or film brought into a warm room will form condensation and result in flat, thin, diffused negatives. The time is now 2:30, so let's go. . . .

Up the steps and into the bride's house. How do you announce yourself? You don't. "The photographer is here!" What do you say to put the bride (and yourself) at ease? Just, "Hello, you look lovely." See how simple it is.

"Now, Miss Bride, let's take the mirror shot."

This is the first of fifteen shots the candid wedding photographer takes at the bride's house for full coverage. They are listed below to give you an idea

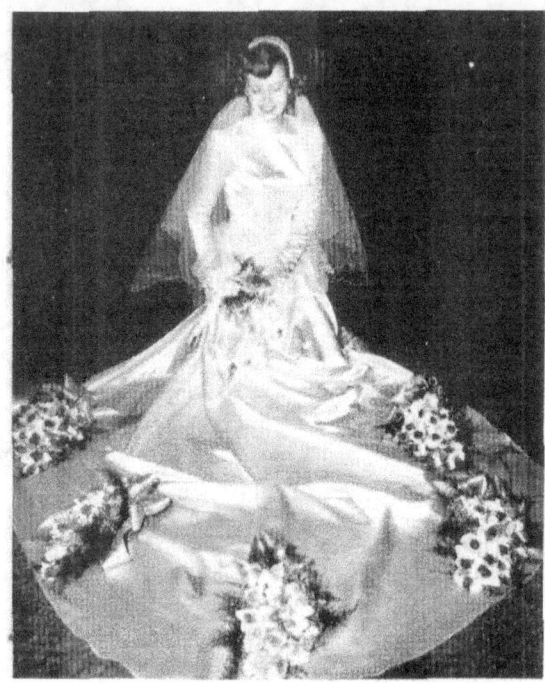 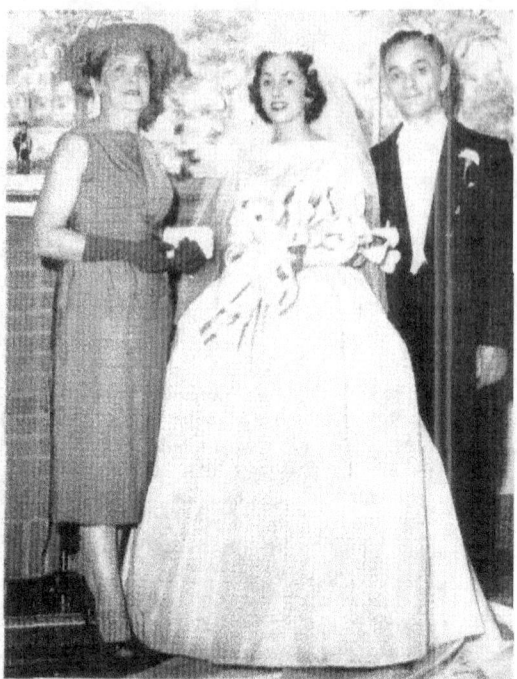

of the pictures you should make. But of greater importance *all* the posing and "how-to" information you will need on the scene accompanies the actual photographs in this book.

Actually the pictures in this book which cover a complete wedding are laid out in sequence, along with full captions. The reason: so this book can serve as an "on-the-job" reference. For example, if you're about to shoot the formal of the bride with her parents (situation nine on the list), all you need is to turn to the proper illustration and you will discover all die material you need to help you pose, light and take the picture. Imitate where possible the composition of each picture. Later when shooting has become automatic, the approach to these shots will be yours, and the style emerging, your own.

Pictures to Take at the Bride's House

1. Mirror Shot of the Bride Alone.
2. Mirror Shot With Maid-of-Honor Assisting.
3. Bride Putting on Blue Garter.
4. Bride Coming Down Stairs.
5. Bride Looking At Her Gifts.
6. Full and Three-Quarter Length Portraits.
7. Bride Sitting on Floor.
8. Bride Pinning Flowers On Mother and Father.
9. Formal of Bride with Parents.
10. Parents Kissing Bride.
11. Informal Shot of Bride with Parents.
12. Bride With Maid-of-Honor.
13. Bride With All Attendants.
14. Bride Leaving House.
15. Bride With Father in Car.

10. *Bride sitting on floor. This picture is impressive with gowns that have a generous train. Have bride kneel three-quarters to camera (instead of actually sitting) then sit back on her heels. If plain wall is not available, place bride before dark background, eliminate detail while printing by fiashing-in. (Busch Pressman; Tri-X; No. 5 bulb; 1/200 at f/19.)* 11. *Formal of bride with parents. Shoot this full-length to show mother and father in their finery. Have parents on either side, preferably turned three-quarters towards bride but with faces toward camera. For intimate mood, bride can be holding one or both parents by the hand. For less formal pose, show group sitting. (Rolleiflex; Tri-X; 60 w/s electronic flash; 1/250, f/8.)*

A Word on Manners and Such

Since it is customary for the bride to arrange for the photographer to have dinner at the reception, avoid bringing anyone with you to the bride's house. This might give the impression that two men are working and put her to the expense and inconvenience of arranging for another dinner. If more than one man is needed to cover the wedding, be sure to inform the bride at the time the wedding is booked.

The candid wedding photographer is at the wedding to work; he is not a guest. If he wears a dark suit, white shirt and conservative tie, he will be appropriately dressed for *any* assignment.

You will have to cope with "nerves," hilarity, confusion, unsolicited advice, high "spirits" and other headaches. Be a gentleman, but when necessary, firm; you will be remembered mostly for your pictures!

There is only one way to cover a candid wedding successfully. Keep your senses right side up! At the house, gracefully refuse any drinks you are offered. At the reception, limit your drinking to a cocktail or two. You have your business reputation to consider. Your conduct should be above reproach.

Equipment for the House Shots

What equipment should you take with you to the bride's house? Everything you'll need for the entire wedding through the reception itself. This means taking all the cameras, film, bulbs or electronic flash units you'll need as you take off for the bride's house. You'll find a full discussion of equipment for candid weddings in chapters 6, 7, and 8, where 4x5, $2^1/4$x2^1A, 35mm and other film sizes are covered in relation to the needs of the candid wedding photographer.

2. CHURCHES AND CEREMONIES

The three religious ceremonies the candid wedding photographer is most apt to shoot are: Protestant, Catholic and Jewish. Though all do contain rituals individual in character, the general pattern of procedure is the same: bride coming up the aisle, altar shots, placing of the ring, benediction, kissing, and couple returning down the aisle.

Catholic

Catholic weddings usually take place between 2:00 P.M. and 5:00 P.M. In the Catholic religion there is also the Nuptial Mass, a wedding ceremony performed before the start of the regular church service, as a rule between 9:00 A.M. and twelve noon. After the wedding the couple remain in the sanctuary during the entire Mass. The couple are in church for the greater part of an hour.

Once the wedding ceremony is over and the regular service has begun, respect the sanctity of the church and the privacy of the worshippers by discontinuing the use of flash. You have already taken your altar shots. The only need to use flash again in the church proper is when the couple return down the aisle.

How often have you wished you were not so pressed by time so you could take the experimental shots you've always wanted to do. Well, the time is now—one-half hour of it! The Nuptial Mass offers a wealth of opportunity to give vent to any artistic impulses you've been harboring. During the Mass the couple kneel before prayer benches for long periods. This is an ideal opportunity for time exposures. For dramatic effect these available light photographs cannot be surpassed.

The outline that follows includes the shots that are taken in both Protestant and Catholic (regular ceremony and nuptial Mass) weddings. Situations occurring only in Catholic weddings are marked with an *.

Church Shots: Protestant and Catholic

1. Bride and Father Walking Away From Car.
2. Bride With Father Walking Up Church Steps.
3. Waiting At the Vestibule.
4. Groom And Best Man Waiting.
5. Coming Up Aisle With Father.
∘6. Father Kissing Bride Just Before Giving Her To The Groom.
7. Bride And Groom Reach The Altar.
8. Shot From Floor Of Aisle.
9. Balcony Shot.
10. Placing Ring On Bride's Or Groom's Finger.
∘11. Kneeling Before Prie-Dieux. (Prayer Benches.) (Nuptial Mass.)
12. Couple Kissing At Altar.
13. Couple Leaving Altar.
14 Coming Down Aisle.
15. Couple Kissing Upon Reaching End of Aisle. (Do not take if they kiss at altar.)
16. Receiving Guests.
17. Couple With Clergyman.
18. Leaving Church.
19. Kissing in Car.
20. Other Car Photos.
21. Looking Through Rear Car Window.
22. Over-All Shot Of The Church From Across The Street.

Note: Most photographers do not shoot the ushers and bride's attendants in the processional march. As the bridal party is photographed in the formals, these half dozen or more shots are seldom included in the album. On the other hand, it pays to take the flower girl or ringbearer. Their photos are too "cute" to resist.

Protestant Variations

Insofar as the candid wedding photographer is concerned, the Protestant and Catholic service is very similar. The obvious differences are: In the Catholic wedding the father kisses the bride before giving her to the groom; in the Protestant, he does not. In the Catholic church the couple walk to the altar where the service takes place; in the Protestant, the service is performed before the altar railing, except when the church has an open chancel. (This is the space including the pulpit, separated from the auditorium by a rail.) Kissing by the couple at the end of the wedding is decided by the individual Catholic church; in the Protestant, kissing is customary. The distance in the Catholic church from railing to altar is much deeper than in most Protestant churches. All in all these are minor differences and the photographer familiar with one service will have no problem with the other.

Jewish Variations

Judaism contains three religious groupings: the Orthodox, Conservative, and Reform. In the traditional Jewish ceremony, the wedding can take place in either the Synagogue or in an establishment that can accommodate the entire affair: cocktails, ceremony and reception. The wedding can take place on any day other than Holy Days or the Sabbath (Friday sundown through Saturday sundown). There is a canopy over the platform on which the ceremony is conducted. It symbolizes the sky. The platform may be decorated with flowers to form a bower. The shots to take are:

1. The ushers advance in pairs and divide, forming a line facing each other on either side of the aisle.
2. The Rabbi comes down the aisle to the altar. He may be chanting a psalm.
3. Best man advances to the altar.
4. Groom comes to the altar escorted by his parents.
5. Maid-of-Honor (or Matron) marches to the altar.
6. Bride is escorted halfway up the aisle.
7. The groom walks down the aisle to meet his bride and escort her to the altar.
8. Bride's parents follow to the altar.
9. The couple's sipping of the wine over which a benediction was re cited by the rabbi.
10. Placing the ring on the bride's finger.
11. The benediction.
12. Smashing of the glass under the groom's heel. (This denotes the destruction of the temple.)
13. Couple kissing.
14. Couple coming down the aisle.
15. Receiving the guests.

As the ushers are photographed in the bridal party formals, each pair of ushers advancing up the aisle often is not included in the album. There are usually three to six pairs of ushers, so ask the bride if she wishes you to take these shots. But once the ushers are in position, shoot all the aisle shots that follow.

Except in the Reform group, it is required that all male heads be covered during the wedding ceremony. Near the door to the chapel there will be a table on which there are skullcaps used for this purpose. You will be handed one. If you are not of this faith, wear the skullcap nevertheless, to respect this tradition.

Ceremony at the Bride's Home

The bride and groom of any faith may prefer the intimacy of a wedding service performed at home and witnessed by those close to them.

In character and sequence the photos taken differ little from those of a church wedding. The bride is photographed as she enters, then several shots are taken during the ceremony, and later the ring shot, kissing, receiving of the guests, the receipt of the marriage certificate and any others you feel the couple may want.

At this type of wedding you may be standing as close as ten feet from the bridal couple. You will capture nuances of expression that are missed at the longer distances of a church wedding. These intimate, emotional glimpses are wonderfully rewarding and will be treasured by all.

The exposures for a home wedding are the same as for the house shots that preceded. If the ceiling is light and no higher than 10 feet I would take a ceremony such as this with partial bounce and include several slow exposures or available light shots. The 35mm camera with an f/2 or faster lens is a natural for available light. A wide-angle lens is perfect for close quarters. Partial bounce with Tri-X and an 80-watt-second electronic flash will call for about an f/5.6; and with a 100-watt-second unit or No. 5 bulb, about f/8.

Restrictions

Catholic: Most Catholic churches permit pictures to be taken during the ceremony. Be sure not to go beyond the altar railing or sacristy door (room adjoining the altar).

How are you to know which Catholic church permits pictures and which does not? The church is fully aware that almost every wedding will have a photographer. If they have any restrictions the bride and groom are told at the time the church arrangements are made. And, as a rule, there is a church attendant or sexton at the door to tell you exactly what their rules are. Whatever the rules, *obey them!* Most restrictions are the result of "wise-guys" who sneak in that extra shot they are told not to take. No professional is ever guilty of such conduct. Aside from the fact that he may have another wedding at this same church tomorrow, the good will he creates is part of photography's public relations. Candid weddings are his bread and butter.

If for any reason you have neglected to ask the bride concerning restrictions and if no one stops you at the door, go ahead and shoot. The photographer, today, is a familiar and accepted part of most weddings. The popping of a flashbulb is hardly noticed. Enthusiastic relatives and friends often shoot more flash than the photographer.

Protestant: Almost without exception, available light shots and time exposures from the balcony or rear of the church are permitted once the couple has reached the altar. Flash shots are not permitted during the ceremony but can be taken when the couple kiss. The general practice is to stage the altar shots after the guests have left the church. The sexton or minister will usually tell you this as you come into the church.

The only shots you will not have taken during the ceremony are the ring shot and the benediction. When staging there is no objection to your standing at the altar so that the couple's faces can be seen. But try to shoot somewhat parallel to the pews, so that the empty pews are not included. It is also most important to point out to the party that their expressions be as serious as they were during the actual ceremony. If the photographer handles this staging correctly, the pictures will look as if they were taken during the service. (This is an excellent time to take formals of the bride, bride and groom, and bridal party, with the altar as a beautiful background.)

Jewish: The only restrictions that may be encountered are during an Orthodox ceremony. In the Conservative and Reform groups if there are any restrictions they will usually come from the bridal couple, and you will be informed as to their nature.

3. FORMALS

Formals are, as the word says, a straight-forward formal recording of the bridal couple and their attendants as they appear on the wedding day. In Catholic and Protestant weddings these formals are always taken after the wedding ceremony, usually at one of the following locations:

1. Church altar, church vestibule, church front or church grounds.
2. Bride's or groom's living room or garden.
3. Park.
4. Hotel lobby or reception hall.

Often there is a break of several hours between church and reception. In order not to be on the job more than is necessary I suggest the first three locations be used soon after the ceremony. This will leave you free until reception time.

You may have planned outdoor formals only to find it raining. Some church vestibules have beautiful wrought iron or wooden doors, or stained glass windows. These provide backgrounds ideal in character for bridal formals. If the couple is concerned about the people waiting outside in the rain, they might concede to the short time it takes to photograph the bride, then bride and groom, only. Groups and family pictures can be taken later at another location.

The fourth location can be used following the ceremony. If this is not convenient, arrange to have the bridal party arrive at the hall one-half hour before reception time so formals can be taken without the disturbing interruptions of well-meaning guests. In the hotel or reception hall there is usually a generous choice of suitable backgrounds for formals: staircase, fireplace,

12. *The bride pinning flowers on her mother is another variation which may be included in the album. Pose the parent so the flowers are visible to the camera. This shot may be either three-quarter or full-length. If the parents' faces are wrinkled or have double chins, shoot from full-length distance, use direct flash to minimize lines. (Busch Pressman; Tri-X; 60 w/s electronic flash; 1/200, f/11; DK-50.) 13. In shot of parents kissing the bride have them touch lips close to her ears so her face will not be hidden. A three-quarter length cropping will eliminate most extraneous matter but do not move in too close as this will introduce distortion. (Minolta Autocord; Tri-X; 60 w/s electronic flash, partial bounce, 1/200, f/5.6; Microdol.) 14. This picture of the bride and her attendants is intended to show the girls in all their splendor. (Remember the bouquets!) The individuals should all be posed at a three-quarter angle to the camera. Partial bounce may be used but reasonable depth-of-field is necessary. You will probably need a No. 5 or No. 8 bulb or an 80-100 w/s electronic flash with the camera stopped down to f/5.6 or f/8. (Busch Pressman; Tri-X; 80 w/s electronic flash, 1/200, f/11; development in DK-50.) 15. This indicates one of the many poses possible of the bride with members of her family. (Minolta Autocord; Tri-X; 80 w/s electronic flash, partial bounce, 1/200, f/5.6; Microdol.)*

drapes or paneled walls. If none are to be found, any simply decorated or painted wall will do. For the formals to take see page 21.

With Jewish weddings, the case is slightly different. Sometimes formals are made before the ceremony, sometimes afterwards. It depends on whether the wedding takes place in an establishment that accommodates the whole affair—cocktails, ceremony and reception, or in a Synagogue. If the wedding does take place in a Synagogue, usually the formals are taken after the ceremony either before or during the reception. The locations: the vestibule of the Synagogue or the grounds outside; or as with Catholic and Protestant weddings, the bride's or groom's living room or garden, a park, or the hotel lobby or reception hall.

When the entire affair takes place in one establishment, formals can often be made before the ceremony, since many brides of Jewish faith do not object to seeing the groom before they actually become man and wife. Suggest this to the bride and groom to be. In most cases they'll be glad to get the formals over with before the ceremony starts. Allow at least fifteen to twenty minutes for picture taking. The hats which are part of customary male attire may either be held or worn. Ask the couple which they prefer.

On Shooting Formals

The import of formals is not understood by many candid wedding photographers. Within one generation the pendulum has swung from one extreme to the other. Studio formals, once represented by faces molded into expressionless masks by competent but overzealous retouchers now have reached the opposite end of the scale: the product of today's quasi-professional whose work is devoid of any ability other than that needed for the making of a straight print.

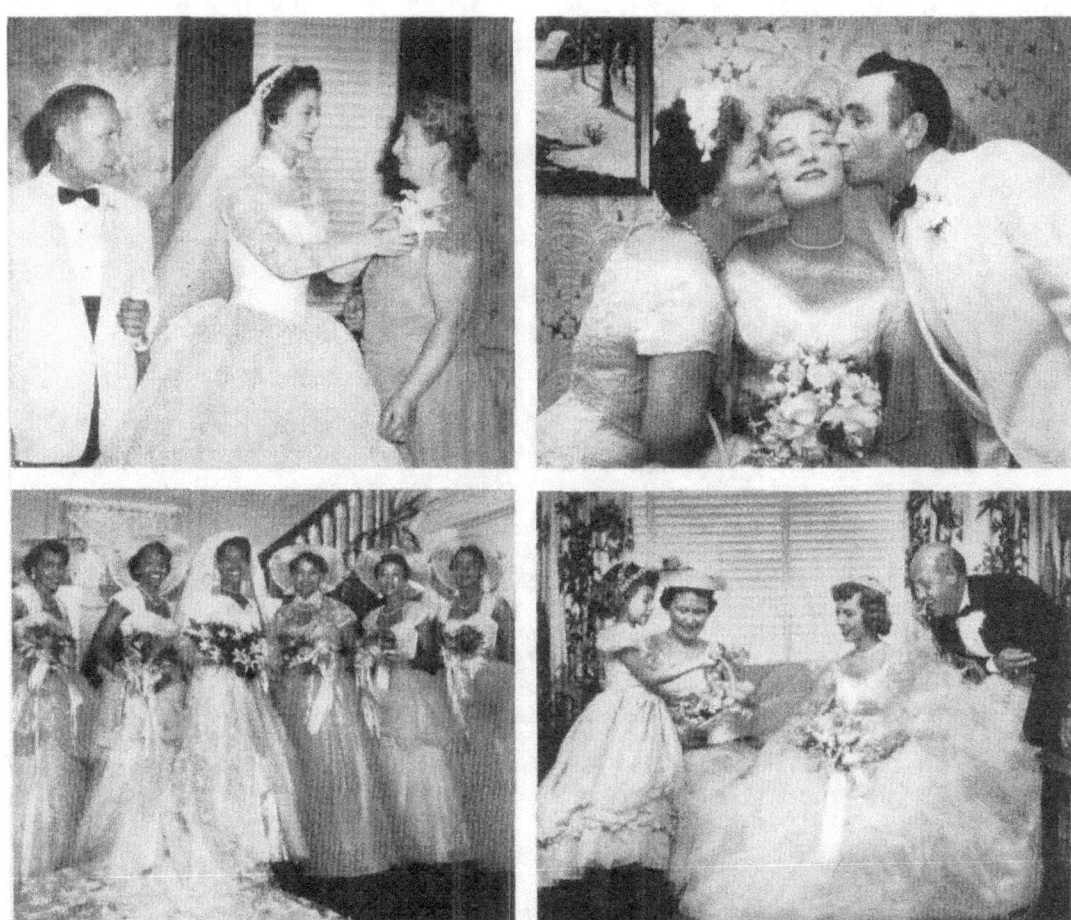

The candid man is not expected to possess the skill of a portrait artist. But he is required to possess the minimal ability needed to restore people to what they really are to the eye; to control what is overemphasized by the searching lens of the camera: recessed or missing teeth, skin blemishes. He should be able to pose his subjects gracefully and without distortion; to arrange their attire attractively and impart the quality of dignity that is an integral part of formal wedding photographs. These are the formals to take:

1. Bride Alone.
2. Bride and Groom, Full-Length.
3. Bride and Groom, Three-Quarter Length.
4. Bridal Party (several shots: see below).
5. Family Groups (several shots: see below).

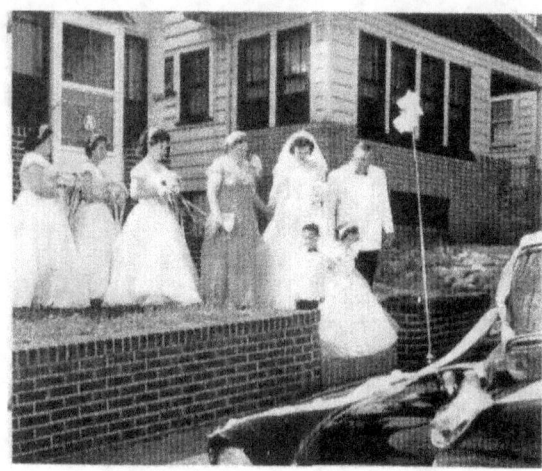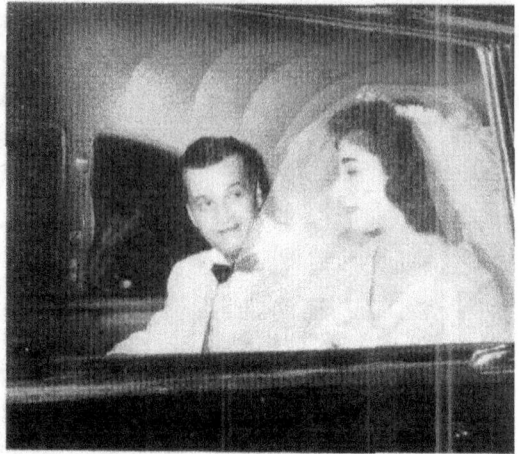

16. *As bride and her party leave the house pose them about 20 feet from the camera. Instruct them to start for their cars when you give the word but not to look at the camera. Expose for daylight. If you use flash fill-in there is no danger of the bulb overpowering the sunlight. (Minolta Autocord; Verichrome Pan; 80 w/s electronic flash, 1/100, f/11; D-76.)* 17. *Bride and father together in the car make an excellent album shot. In colder weather, this shot may have to be taken through a closed window. To eliminate reflection of the flash in the glass shoot at an angle of at least 20°. Be careful of reflections of the scenery which may show in a closed window. (Retina Ha; Plus-X; 80 w/s electronic flash, 1/200, f/11; Microdol.)*

For formal shots of the bride alone, and those of bride and groom, take at least three exposures of each formal (two full-length, and one three-quarters). At least two exposures of the bridal party should be made.

The next five (or six) photos can be taken at this time, or if all the subjects are not present, left to the reception.

1. Bride and groom with maid-of-honor and best man.
2. Bride and groom with her parents.
3. Bride and groom with his parents (or all parents may be included in
   one picture).
4. Bride and groom with all her family.
5. Bride and groom with all his family.
6. Bride and groom with grandparents.

Formals should be taken front-face for that is how we think of people close to us and not in terms of three-quarter view or profile. This is not to say that the subject may not be flattered by turning the head a little to one side.

Hold It!

Remember formals are "a straight-forward recording." The object—particularly in groups—is to have the subjects looking directly at you with relaxed expressions and most important, with their *eyes open*. Keep their attention with pleasant chatter, Just before you shoot, in a strong, staccato voice, shout, "Hold it!" And they will! Their eyes will focus on you, open and alert, long enough to take the picture. Say what you will against, "Hold it!" I use it—and closed eyes with me are a rarity. I know photographers who just shoot; they consistently come back with a number of negatives ruined by closed eyes. Unless you are willing to double the number of exposures to insure good formals, hold their attention with—"Hold it!"

A Special Case

Talking of formals—one thing we've omitted is the "studio formal" for the newspaper story about the wedding. If the story is to appear in a big city paper, then the picture must be taken in advance and delivered to the newspaper some two to three weeks before publication date. With small town newspapers, there's more leeway. Often such a paper will hold the story till a picture from the candid wedding coverage is available. The bride's picture for the paper does not need to be glossy. A fine grain paper will do equally well; besides it is easier to retouch. (See Retouching, Chapter 10.)

Naturally this shot should be a head and shoulders pose, unless the bride assures you that she can get a three-quarter length pose into the paper. This applies specifically to big city papers where space is at a premium. Small town papers are usually more liberal with their space and frequently will include a full-length portrait. A phone call to the local society editor will give you all the answers you need on specific rulings and deadlines for these "studio formals." This is information you should have at your fingertips.

Shooting "Studio Formals"

Even an experienced studio portrait man who is skilled in posing, lighting and retouching, and capable of producing a good negative and print, finds it impossible to satisfy with every formal portrait sitting.

"All brides are beautiful," is a pleasant platitude that is used glibly by everyone. The photographer soon finds, all brides are not! If you do not possess some knowledge of the skills mentioned, don't look for trouble. Avoid portraits and stick to candid weddings. The best solution is to tie in with a local studio and send them the brides who request formal studio portraits or pictures for the paper. This way you will also be secure in knowing that the studio which does your brides' portraits will not attempt to get your candid. If you decide to do your own wedding portraits, here are some suggestions.

The candid photographer with a 4x5 or 3y4x4y4 camera plus the lens used for weddings, is equipped to take standing or three-quarter length portraits. If the negative is well filled, three-quarter length portraits with the bride sitting may have some distortion of the lower part of the gown and of the hands and bouquet if they are not close to the body. This can be corrected satisfactorily during enlargement by raising the lower end of the easel.

In portrait photography, it is particularly important to fill your negative completely. With a normal length lens it is difficult to do this without distortion, except for profiles. The 4x5 camera with a double-extension bellows is limited to about 9-inch lens for portraits of this composition; with a triple-extension bellows a 12-inch lens is suggested. The longer focal-length, instead of the standard focal-length lens, is to be preferred for three-quarters, and wherever feasible for full-length bridals; it will help minimize distortion and produce a more pleasing perspective.

For the photographer with a press-type bellows camera who shoots just an occasional wedding and who does not feel the expense of another lens is warranted, an inexpensive supplementary telephoto attachment, such as the Telek, is the answer. It will provide the general advantages of a longer focal-length lens. The use of a supplementary telephoto attachment necessitates the use of a longer bellows extension and results in a decrease in effective lens aperture (longer than normal exposures). The Kodak Master Photoguide will indicate the exposure adjustment needed for your particular focal-length lens with extra attachment. Some aberration is introduced by the telephoto attachment but an f/8 or smaller opening will restore definition.

A 21/4x21/4 negative demands superlative retouching; a 21/4x23/4 very much the same. The only recourse for the photographer with a small camera, is to use an inexpensive 4x5 or 5x7 view camera, (with the minimum of distortion controls) that will take up to a 9- or 12-inch lens. Unless contact prints are sufficient for his purposes, he will need an enlarger for the larger negative size. No economy is possible here because the quality of the print is determined by the quality of the enlarging equipment.

4. THE RECEPTION AND AFTERWARDS

With house and church shots we have had to contend with deadlines, but at the reception the pressure is off. There is not the worry of missing an important shot. Unlike the wedding ceremony, pictures may be spaced or posed at the photographer's discretion.

What to Take

You take the same pictures regardless of the size of the hall or the elaborateness of the affair. This holds true even if the reception should be at home. The order of the outline (below) does not necessarily have to be followed in sequence. *AH* of the shots do not have to be taken—in fact sometimes they *cannot* be taken. But the outline shown follows along the way a reception progresses.

But before you start be sure you have the right equipment. Use of cameras from 35mm to 4x5 for candid weddings is discussed fully in chapters 6, 7, and 8. Chapter 3 goes into using available light, while chapter 4 deals exclusively with flash and electronic flash. Good reception pictures can be taken with all of the camera sizes mentioned, with flashbulbs or electronic flash and even by available light.

Personally, when I cover a reception, I take two Rolleis with Rollei-meters. The twenty-four exposures often are enough for all my reception shots. The Rollei's (almost) fully automatic features make working a pleasure. I also take a "35," preferably with a fast 35mm lens. I use the Ultra blitz Matador I electronic flash (135-watt sec.) at one-half power for most of my straight flash shots up to 15 feet, and full power for distances beyond.

Pictures to Take at the Reception and Afterwards

1. Couple Entering Reception.
2. Couple Dancing.
3. Couple Being Toasted.
4. Couple Toasting Each Other.
5. Couple Kissing.
6. Couple Showing Bride's Ring.
7. Cutting The Cake.
8. Bride Feeding Cake to Groom. Groom Feeding Cake to Bride.
9. Reception Hall. (Available Light; Flash)
10. Garter Shot.
11. Bride Scolding the Groom.
12. Bride Kissing the Groom's Friend.
13. Bride Throwing Bouquet.
14. Bride and Groom Sneaking Away.
15. Waving Goodbye From Their Car.
16. Placing Shoes Outside Hotel Door.
17. Other Shots.

Handling People

Now everybody is relaxed and happy, intent on having a good time. The bride has "got her man" and a rosy glow surrounds them. You will have to break through that haze to come up with pictures. Have no qualms about this—that's why you're here. Make your point, but if they object to any particular shot—forget it. I have had brides who, although they would have liked to include a bouquet throwing shot, were not willing to disrupt the festivities by assembling all the girls. The final decision on the taking of any shot should rest with the couple. Here they come! Let's get that happy look on film.

Aside from the list given, there are other reception pictures you should take which will increase your sales. These vary greatly depending on the nationality of the couple being married. For example, at Polish wedding receptions frequently the bride takes her veil off and pins it on the maid-of-honor, to indicate that she is next. Also at Polish weddings, the bride's mother proffers salt, bread and wine to the couple to denote that they are starting married life with the bitter and the sweet. They dip the bread in salt and taste it, then sip the wine. A little research on your part will easily bring to light any customs which would make good candid wedding picture material. Be prepared also to shoot interesting folk dances at the reception, such as the Polish Polka, the Greek, Italian and Jewish dances.

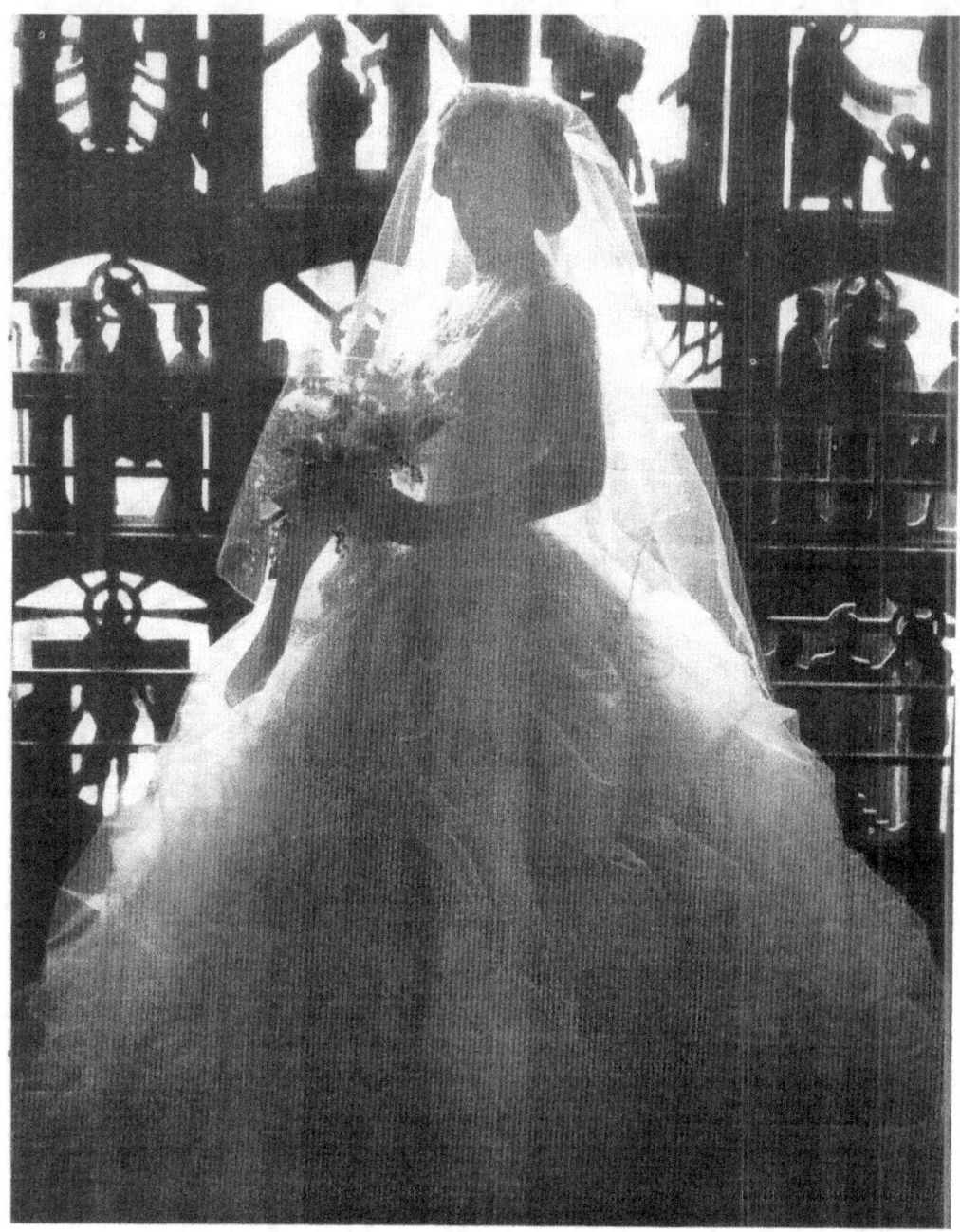

18. *To keep within my quota of 60 shots I generally do not photograph the bride alone waiting in the vestibule, hut this beautiful wrought-iron church door cried for a silhouette. The exposure was by guess: 1/125, f/5.6 on Tri-X film (Rolleiflex). Negative treated in Victor intensifier to improve detail and contrast. Printed on DuPont Varigam without a filter and detail hurned-in on flowers and right shoulder through a No. 3 filter. Ferricyanide solution applied to face to bring out a suggestion of features.*

3

Available Light Photography

" A VAILABLE LIGHT" is a relatively new expression that has been added to the photographer's vocabulary. Unfortunately, the term lacks crystallization, and definitions are both varied and contradictory. Interpretations have been expressed that encompass the extremes of sunlight and match light! The confusion, I believe, originated from the all-inclusive name—"available light" or light that is available for picture taking.

Certainly a "daylight exposure" is taken with light that is available, but it is called a daylight exposure with such refinements as sunny, cloudy, open shade etc. It has never been nor need ever be called available light. Certainly a quarter second, a full second, or any exposure too long for the camera to be hand-held is defined most explicitly as a "time-exposure" and not available light. Up to this point almost everyone is in agreement. But take the case of a subject photographed at 1/50 and f/5.6 by daylight coming through a window and the camp is divided. Some will insist it is an available light shot. I'm puzzled. How does it differ from the picture taken under the shade of a porch or tree? What, suddenly, has caused the one to be available light and the other a daylight (open shade) exposure? The light source? Direction of light? Exposure? Availability? No, they are all alike.

What Is Available Light?

"Available," "existing," or "found light" began appearing along with the introduction of fast films and super-speed developers. With the addition of Kodak's Tri-X (pushed beyond normal limitations) the popularity of these terms took fire but not direction.

The first to use these expressions were the white-haired, f/1.4 to f/2 boys with their high-octane developers—the boys who came back with a picture where no picture could be gotten. There is no question in my mind that to these pioneers the only differentiation between a one second f/4.5 "time-exposure" and a 1/25, f/2 (forced development) "available light" shot—identical in point-of-view and illumination—was in the simple act of picking up the camera. But with this simple act the rules of cause and effect went into play. Cause: the 1/25 sec. hand-held exposure. Effect: the need for fast lenses, fast

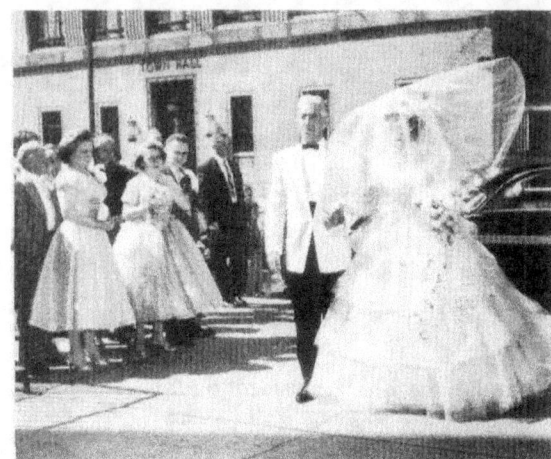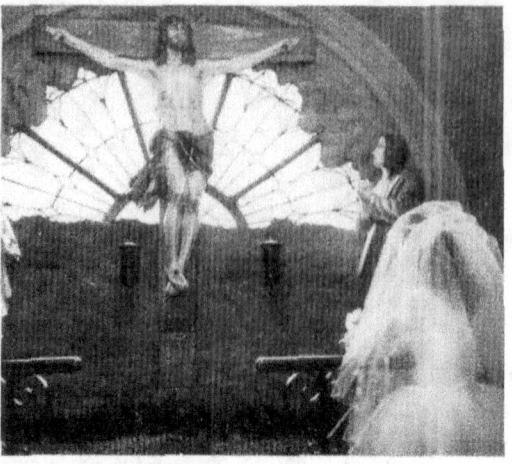

19. As *the bride and her father walk from the car to the church, shoot at a distance of about 15 feet (20 feet with a 35mm camera and 50mm lens). Set your camera for this distance and for daylight exposure. Wait until the bride's gown is arranged and they start forward. If necessary, walk backward to maintain distance until everything is perfect. On cloudy days or in open shade forget the fill-in flash. (Rolleiflex; Verichrome Pan; 80 w/s electronic flash, 1/200, f/11; D-76.)* 20. *This vestibule picture of the kneeling bride was a "grab shot." It might have been effective and dramatic without a fill-in flash but the picture I saw was soft and the mood was quiet so I used weak bounce fash. (Rolleiftex; Tri-X; 1/30, f/4, 60 w/s electronic flash.)*

film, powerful developers. In other words, the simple act effected a departure from the accepted rules and tools of photography and provided the freedom of movement through which the camera could speak with greater eloquence. Also, in my mind, there is no question that an available light assignment meant low light level conditions: either flash or flood was prohibited, or retaining naturalness or mood was desired.

This, I believe, is what was meant by available light. Today, it means this and very much more. Kodak in their pamphlet, "Kodak Tri-X Roll Film—Its Use and Characteristics," referring to "Available Light" states: "In brightly lighted interiors of schools, gymnasiums, cafeterias, stores, industrial and commercial interiors, art galleries, museums, exhibitions, etc. pictures have been made at exposures of 1/100 at f/5.6" and it continues ". . . negatives given the normal development."

Films the speed of Kodak Tri-X, Ilford HPS, and DuPont SX are responsible for this welcome confusion. They have pushed back the barriers and greatly extended photography's potential. Pictures once possible only with f/1.4 or f/2 lenses could be taken with an f/2.8 or f/3.5. Dramatic, realistic, natural photographs immediately became popular. They were no longer the envied performance of the few with expensive 35's, but within the scope of the millions with family cameras. A word was needed to explain this new photography, and the old term "available light" was appropriated. I think the term, "found light," would have been more to the point and less controversial. The vagaries of nomenclature are beyond comprehension: bulb means lamp; strobe, electronic flash; and soup, developer. So long as we all have a good idea of what we are talking about the term is unimportant and "available" light will do.

But in (mis)appropriating the term, available light, we have left our white-haired boys—still pioneering—in the dark. An expression that can not be compromised must be found to define what magic they are brewing with super-fast f/1.1 lenses, flickering candlelight, mystery soups and their "black cat in a coal bin." Of late the term "low light level" has been appearing in our photography magazines. It is an expression that leaves no room for confusion. It will serve our pioneers admirably.

Now for an argument that is reminiscent of pictorialist versus purist: should we take our available light straight, or mixed with flood, flash, reflector, etc. The topic can provide hours of amateur bull sessions but does not pay the professional's rent. With experience we become masters of equipment and material. At the moment of shooting, the photographer is the only judge of what will make a natural picture. A church balcony shot can be made more natural by adding a fill-in flash to a slow exposure. An available light photo of a bride taken by the light of an open window (I have conformed) will look more true if either a reflector, a weak bulb or a flash bounced off the farther wall is used to "open up" the shadows. Without the photographer's ingenuity, equipment and material are incapable often of reproducing the effect of the tremendous latitude registered by the perfect camera and film—the eye and the brain.

Having to shoot a complete candid wedding by available light is a remote possibility. Unless the bride or groom are averse to flash the only logical place to expect any restrictions is in the church. Slow exposures are all good and well, but with a 1/25 sec. exposure the shackles are broken: the photographer's movement is unhampered and moderate subject motion can be stopped.

The recent announcement of Kodak's new Royal-X Pan sheet film with its speed ranging from a conservative 750 to a possible 8,000 depending on development, greatly extends the photographer's available light possibilities. Though at this writing the new fast film is available only in sheet film sizes, there is reason to believe that it may become available for smaller cameras.

Available Light Techniques

Fast f/1.4 to f/2.8 lenses, and films with at least the speed of Kodak Tri-X or Ilford HPS are necessary. Medium fine grain, special-purpose developers like FR's X-500 and Ilford Microphen are helpful where poor lighting calls for pushing film to speeds several times above those recommended by the manufacturer. Royal-X Pan can develop remarkable speed in DK-60a or DK-50. In weddings there is a limit. The case is not like photo-reporting where

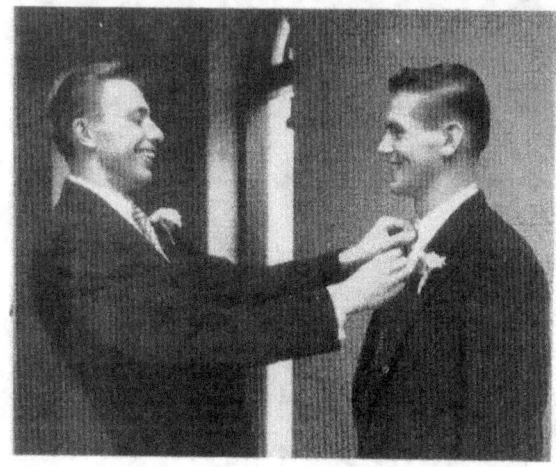

21. *After photographing the bride approaching church, go to the room adjoining the altar to catch the groom and best man. You may also include the clergyman, if present. (Rolleiflex; Verichrome Pan; 80 w/s electronic flash, partial bounce, 1/250, f/5.6; D-76.)*

any photo is better than none. Wedding photos deal with human vanities. The subject must be "shown in a good light."

Fast films plus strong developers equal grain. Obvious grain is foreign to the layman's concept of a good wedding picture. The larger our film the less apparent the graininess. The smaller the diaphragm opening the greater the depth-of-field. Both these physical results can be made to work for us. In most churches, altar pictures can be taken at 1/30 and f/5.6 if film like Tri-X is processed in high-energy developer. This gives us the choice of three cameras: the 35, the roll film camera and the 4x5. The roll film camera is the natural choice. The depth-of-field is considerably better than with the 4x5, and without close scrutiny, graininess is scarcely perceptible. A combination of a 35 at f/1.4 to f/2 with Microdol will give you about the same graininess as roll film (forced) but at the expense of depth of field. Cameras are merely tools. Their productivity is equal only to the ability and resourcefulness of the photographer. (Several of the illustrations show the difference which camera choice can have on the finished picture.)

An accurate light-meter is essential for optimum results. It will help prevent pushing the film more than is necessary. Kodak's Tri-X can safely be rated at the equivalent of 500 to 800 ASA with a 13 minute development at 68 degrees in Microphen, or 11 minutes in X-500, diluted 1:10. Pushing the film beyond 800 is not recommended, but if there is no alternative, develop for 16 minutes or more with Microphen, or about 13 minutes with X-500. Where the accuracy of the exposure is questionable or "pushing" is carried to extremes, the only method for knowing when your film has had enough is through developing by inspection (see Chapter 9).

If you know your meter and how to use it, trust it—not your judgment. Judgment is for times your meter does not register or in situations where it can not be used. Close guessing comes only after considerable experience. With a reflected light meter, take the reading off the palm of your hand; with an incident light meter, place your meter in front of your subject and direct the light gathering sphere or area at your lens.

For house shots, make full use of any daylight that is coming through the windows; learn to use walls, house lights and mirrors as a reflector or fill-in; remove the lampshades and your exposure can jump from 1/5 to 1/25 of a second. A reflector that is easy to handle is a helpful accessory for house shots.

With Tri-X and high energy developers, 1/25 at f/2 is the usual exposure for **aisle** shots and 1/25 at f/5.6 for altar pictures. If a generous amount of daylight is streaming through the windows you have the alternative of a smaller f/stop or **a** faster shutter speed. Reception rooms, though subdued in lighting, should offer easy shooting with an 800 (ASA equivalent) rating.

On occasion there is no choice but to include along with the available-light exposures, daylight shots such as leaving the house or church. These should be given the same rating as the indoor shots. Increasing the shutter speed from a "normal" 1/200 and f/16 for Tri-X in bright sun to 1/400 or 1/500, will take care of the {ASA equivalent) 400; add a K2 (medium yellow) filter and the 800 rating is taken care of.

If indoor flash should be included on the same available light roll, double your shutter speed from your "normal" flash exposure (see Chapter 4) and close down one-half stop for ASA equivalent speed of 400. To increase speed to 800 from the "normal" exposure for flash, double the shutter speed and close down one and a half f/stops.

If a wedding calls for a mixture of flash and available light try to keep each type in a separate magazine. Microdol, (or other fine-grain developers) can then be used with flash, the more potent solutions with available light. Daylight exposures can he shot on your flash magazines.

The reason for shooting a candid is to preserve the highlights of the wedding day. With available light, play it safe. If you are in doubt, take another shot at double the exposure. Shoot a lot, but remember there is a time to stop. Ninety-six shots, including duplicates, will be necessary if you use one 20-shot magazine for house, one for church, one for formals and 36 shots for the reception. Beyond that you will be repeating and if you continue to ask the bride and groom to pose you will cause them to be more annoyed than appreciative.

Color used indoor by available light is too impractical a combination to rely on for a good and complete coverage of a wedding, even with new color film rated at an index of 100 or more. It is a combination that is best avoided— for the present.

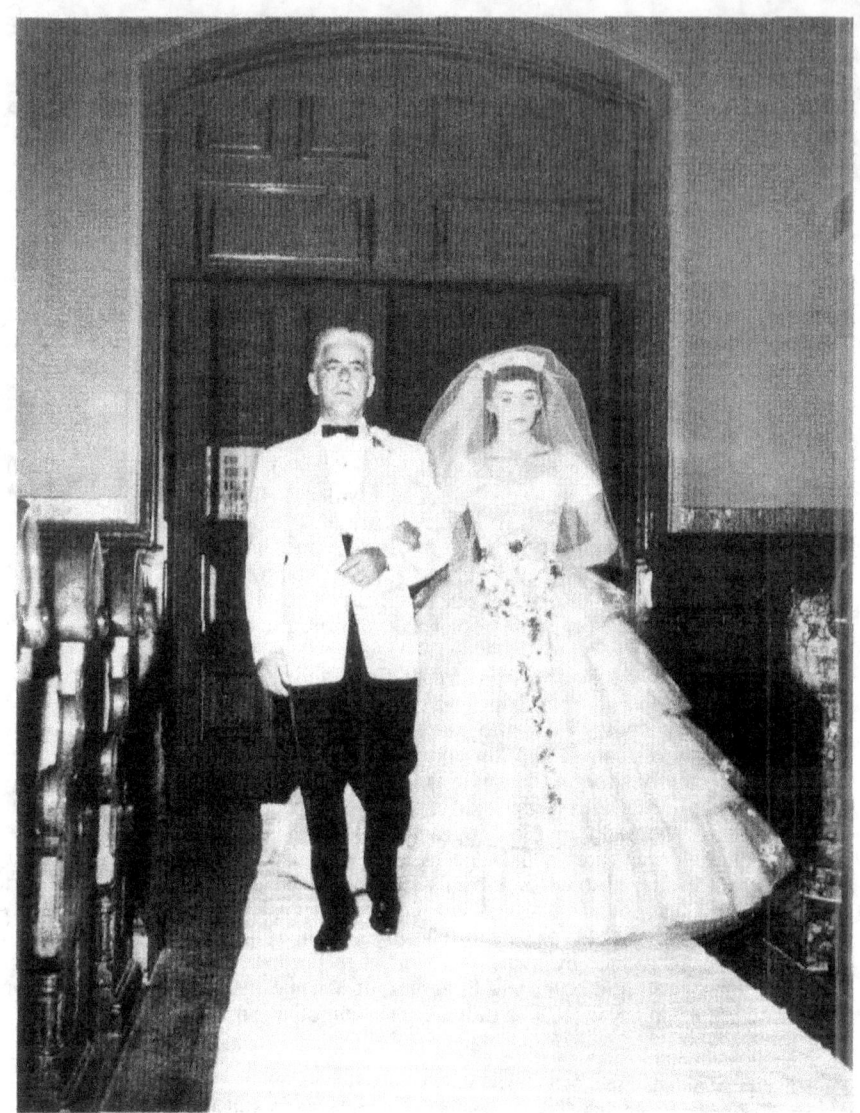

22. *For the photograph of the bride coming up the aisle with her father, set the camera and f/stop for 15 feet. If there are few people near the rear of the church catch the bride and her father near the first pew so it will not look as if the church is empty. By taking this shot toward the back of the church the walls and balcony will register: if there is a black background the bridal couple will almost always find it objectionable. (Mamiya 6; Verichrome Pan; 80 w/s electronic flash unit, 1/200, f/8; film developed in D-76.)*

4.

Flash and Electronic Flash

SOONER on LATER every potential candid wedding photographer faces the same set of problems. Which type of artificial illumination should he use: electronic flash with X-sync or the familiar flashbulb with M-sync? If he chooses electronic flash what factors should be taken into consideration? And how should either type of lighting be used for the best results in candid wedding photography? Before you make any decision (or purchases) let's take a look at the entire situation.

The term "strobe light" for the electronic flash is a misnomer. A strobo-scope is an instrument that interrupts the light at intervals. An appropriate name is the one used by both manufacturers and photo magazines—"speed-light." But the power of the press seems to be waging a losing battle with the power of usage and I believe that "strobe" is here to stay. In this book, however, I will refer to the "speed light" or "strobe," as electronic flash; the "flash-lamp" as a flashbulb or bulb.

In June, 1851 in England, William Henry Fox Talbot made the first photograph by the brief flash of an electric spark. In 1931, improvements made by Dr. Harold E. Edgerton took the one millionth of a second spark out of the category of an intriguing though impractical curiosity and put it into everyday application.

Other improvements followed quickly: Today we have three to five-pound battery-powered units. Electronic flash is the most dramatic flash "discovery" since the introduction of the flashbulb. In professional photography and with candid weddings particularly, it has all but replaced the flashbulb. Indoors, its very short flash duration produces negatives that are devoid of both camera or subject motion. Cost of operation is about three cents per shot for some dry-cell units, to almost no cost at all for the line current studio and home AC units. There are several sources of power: AC electricity (house current), wet and dry-cell batteries, and nickel-cadmium batteries. Some units permit use of both line current and battery. In all, electrical energy is fed into a capacitor and then is discharged through a flashtube containing xenon gas (usually). The result is a flash of very short duration.

23. *The father kisses the bride before giving her to the groom in the Catholic ceremony; in the Protestant service there is no kiss. You may leave your camera focused as for the previous shot (bride and father coming up the aisle) or, if there is time, focus on the subjects, so altar will be clearer. Father handing over bride will probably he the last flash exposure permitted in the Protestant service, but you may be able to re-stage the other important shots after the service is over or use slow exposures for the following shots. (Konica III; Plus-X; No. 5 bulb, 1/200, f/8; Microdol.)* 24. *A shot from the floor in the aisle is best made from about the fifteenth pew back. Focus accurately on the bride and groom. It is easiest to compose this in a reflex camera; with others you may practically have to lie on the floor to see your picture. I get good results by placing the camera on the floor with the front propped up about half an inch with a small object. Do not use flash with this shot. (Mamiya 6; Tri-X; 1 sec., f/4.5; Microdol.)* 25. *This picture (lower left) may be made as the bridal couple advances to the altar and genuflects, or it may be made later in the service. This particular photograph indicates the possibilities of using a hand-held camera and forced negative development under available light conditions. It was made with a Rolleiflex and Tri-X film exposed at 1/30 and f/5.6, forced developed in FR X-500 (diluted 1:10) for 11 minutes.* 26. *When photographing from the balcony, focus on the bridal couple and place the camera on the railing or some other firm support. Wait until the organ stops because vibration will soften the image. This picture was made with a Mamiya 6 using Tri-X film and a combination of a slow exposure (1 sec, f/3.5) and electronic flash. (Flash exposures are often permitted during the Catholic ceremony.)*

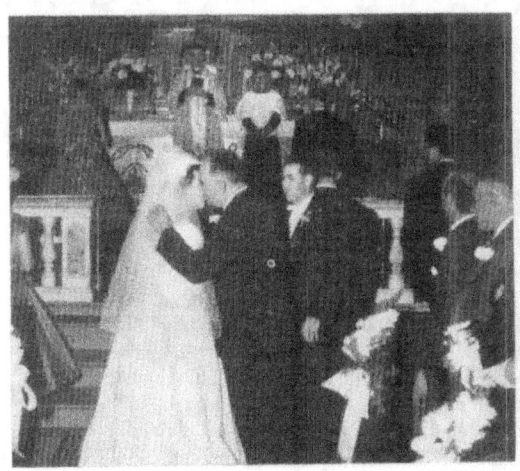
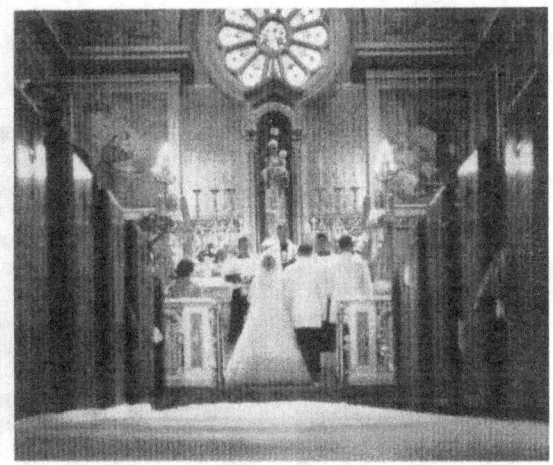
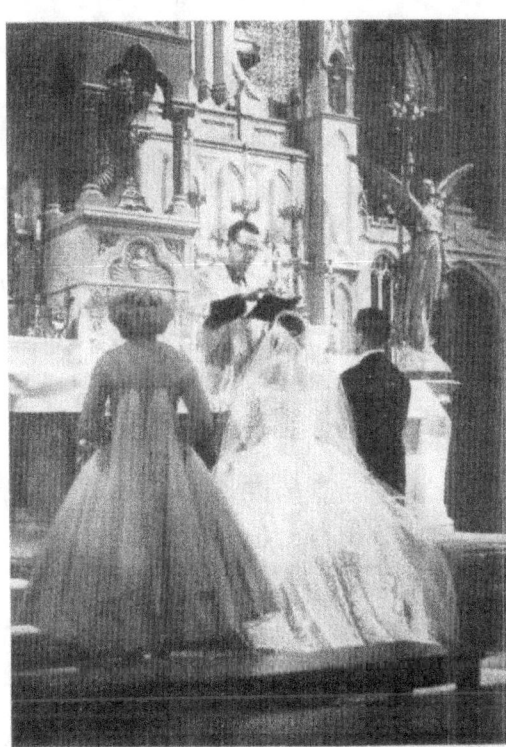
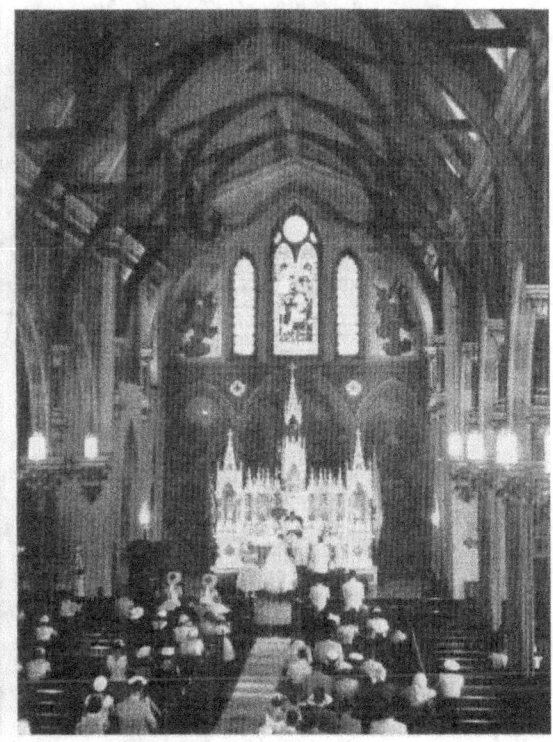

27. This balcony shot in a smaller church was made with available light only (Tri-X, 1 sec. at f/3.5, Microdol) with a Mamiya 6. 28, 29. In many Catholic churches the door to the Sacristy is directly off the altar and so situated that the faces of the bridal couple may be seen from it. From this inconspicuous spot I photographed the bride placing the ring on the groom's finger (upper right) and the couple being blessed with holy water (lower left). Picture 29 was made with flash but you may also try an available light exposure (like 28) for a more dramatic effect. In Protestant services when shots are posed after the ceremony there will be no problem of finding an inconspicuous vantage point (28: Retina IIIc; Tri-X; 1/30, f/4; Microphen; 29: Busch Pressman; Tri-X; 80 w/s electronic flash unit, 1/200, f/8; DK-50.) 30. During the Nuptial Mass, there are long periods without motion which provide excellent opportunities for available light shots. The Prie-Dieux pose, (lower right) was made from the door of the Sacristy. (Busch Pressman; Tri-X; 1/2 second, f/4.7; film developed in DK-50.)

How to Rate Your Electronic Flash

The prevailing practice is to rate electronic flash units by watt-seconds input—in other words, how much energy is transmitted from power pack to flashtube. This rating system is not adequate as it fails to take into account the efficiency of the flashtube and the design and finish of the reflector.

A system has been worked out for standardizing the terminology and method of rating an electronic flash unit. It is based on the amount of light reaching the subject, the area it covers, and the duration of the flash. To put it technically: effective beam candlepower seconds, coverage of the reflector and speed of flash. Until this method of rating an electronic flash is established, the rudimentary expedient of testing by standing three people against a light wall (so that one appears at either end of the viewfinder, and one in the middle) and shooting from about 12 feet away, will serve to determine the output and coverage of a unit.

How to *Find Your Guide Number*

Try this test for rating your unit with camera on a tripod, gun close to camera, reflector parallel to camera front, and room light low. The electronic flash unit (with reasonably fresh or fully charged batteries) should be turned on for about three minutes to make sure the unit is operating at maximum output. Discharge it and let it recharge.

Make the first exposure with No. 5 flashbulb, and camera at 1/10 second (to eliminate possibility of shutter inaccuracy) at the guide number recommended for open flash by the manufacturer of your film. This will be your "normal negative" against which all electronic flash exposures will be matched. The flashbulb reflector should be polished and of a good make. The room light during the exposure, should be out or very low.

Next make one exposure with the electronic flash at a fast shutter speed so room light does not register (about 1/200) using the guide number recom-

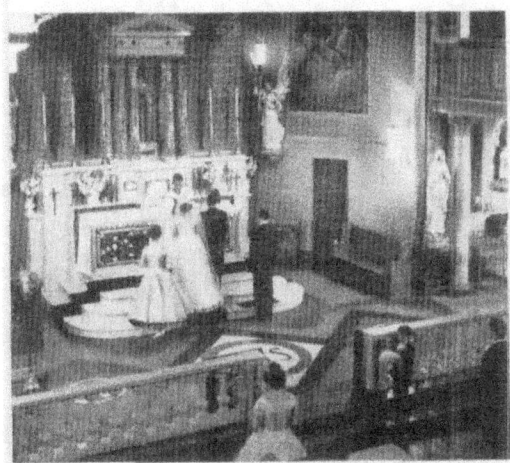 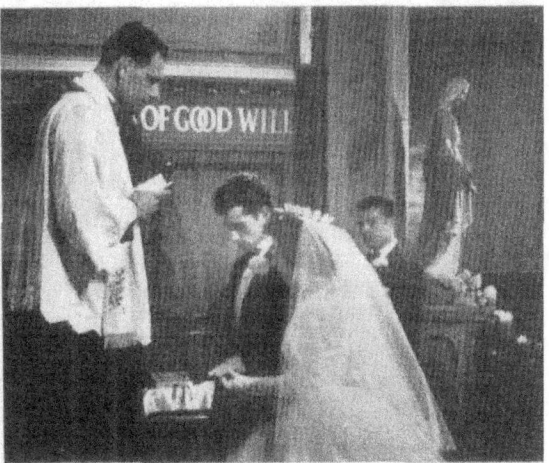

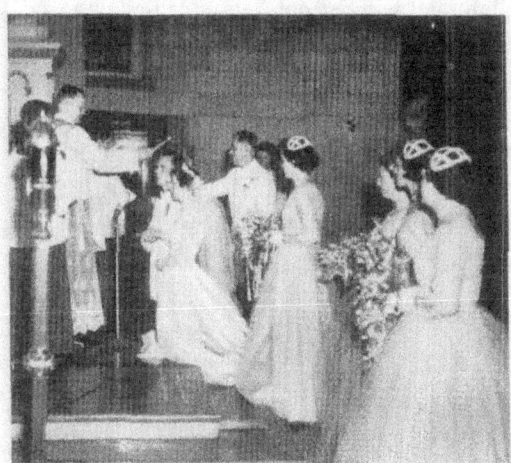 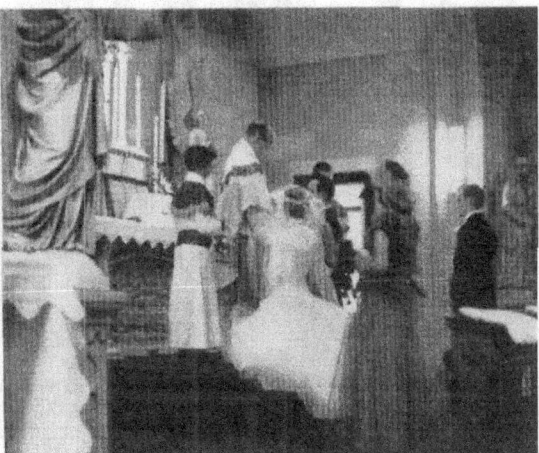

mended by the electronic flash maker: then ten exposures, progressively opening the diaphragm one quarter of an f/stop. Allow at least triple the recommended recycling-time between exposures. Develop all the film in the same developer, at once, for the time and temperature recommended by the film manufacturer on the instruction sheet.

If you're using sheet film, before development clip a corner of the flashbulb negative to identify it. For the electronic flash pictures, be sure to develop film 10 percent more if you're using a unit with a flash duration faster than 1/500 second. To locate the flashbulb exposure on roll film during development, you will have to develop by inspection. Use Kodak Desensitizer and a green Wratten 7 Safelight Filter, or inspect briefly during development (without using the desensitizer) by light from a very dim green safelight (Wratten 3 Safelight Filter). In either case your first, or flashbulb exposure, will be at the taped end of the film. Cut this exposure off. Fix it. Continue developing the rest of the roll.

The electronic flash exposure that most closely matches the flashbulb negative is the one you need for candids. To determine the guide number, multiply the f/stop of the chosen exposure by the number of feet from electronic flash lamp to subject; in this case, 12 feet. If f/11 was the aperture, then: 11 x 12 - 132. If half way between f/11 and f/16, then: 13-5 x 12 -162. That's your guide number.

Here's how to prove the correctness of your electronic flash negative before you settle on a final guide number. Make one straight enlargement from the flashbulb negative, and one from the electronic flash negative. Expose for identical times, at the same f/stop, and from the same enlarger position. The exposure for enlargement (at least 15 seconds) should be such that the flashbulb print is fully developed in the time recommended by the paper manufacturer. Develop both sheets at once and take them out at the same time.

These enlargements, printed straight and without burning-in or dodging, and using the whole negative, will reveal if the flash is distributed evenly over the three people and over the light wall behind them. (Be sure your enlarger light distribution is even.) If your electronic flash negative is right, the density and contrast of the prints should be almost identical—with one exception: an electronic flash exposure on pan film will produce a print with lighter blues (eyes, gowns, etc.), and darker reds (lipstick, freckles, etc.) than a flashbulb shot.

The enlarging chart (Chapter 10) will help you in adjusting the developing time to fit your particular enlarger system.

Buying an Electronic Flash Unit

What kind of electronic flash unit is best suited to candid wedding photography? There are several important considerations: Whether a unit powered by "D" cell photo-flash batteries (giving about 30 to 50 flashes) is compatible with your needs, or you require a high-voltage dry-cell battery unit (some 400 to 800 flashes); the rapidity of the recycling time; if recharging your battery is practical (we'll go into that later). Shelf life is about 6 to 12 months for high voltage dry-cell batteries. The candid wedding photographer shooting often will not want to be bothered with frequent battery changes. In all probability he will choose the electronic flash which provides a large number of flashes per battery, or per charge. A ready-light is a must, not so much to indicate when the unit is charged (most 60-100-watt-second high voltage dry cells, and rechargeable battery units charge between flashes in 3 to 7 seconds) as to warn, by increasingly longer delays, when the life of the battery is nearing its end.

Electronic flash, though efficient, can be considered still in an experimental stage. Improvements are being effected with a rapidity that makes current models seem outdated, sometimes within a matter of months. Basically, however, all electronic flash units are similar and the following paragraphs which include information on three popular portable units I have used should provide some idea of what the uninitiated can expect of the various types of electronic flash units.

Which Type of Electronic Flash Unit?

For the photographer who shoots several candids a month, an electronic flash unit is profitable. The cost of operating the dry-cell Heiland Strobonar V, excluding costs of repairs, is about three cents per shot, for the dry-cell Mighty Light DeLuxe about two cents, and for the wet-cell Ultra blitz Matador I, a fraction of a cent as against eight to ten cents each for the No. 5 or 25 flashbulb. (Amplex has a baseless bulb they rate at 7,500 lumens. It retails for about six cents.) The old 10- to 15-pound portable wet-cell electronic flash has developed into a 2- to 7-pound dry-cell, or rechargeable wet, or nickel-cadmium cell unit. (The nickel-cadmium will give more flashes for each charge than the wet cell.) Studios will pay five to ten cents extra per shot for electronic flash and encourage its use. It eliminates the possibility of camera movement showing in the negative.

The Strobonar V, one of the three dry-cell units I have used, is rated at 80-watt seconds' input. Another is the 60-watt-second (w/s) Mighty Light DeLuxe. Both these units proved reliable and trouble-free. Weight with the Mighty Light DeLuxe is negligible (2 pounds for the battery pack) and it gives roughly 800 shots with each set of batteries, twice as many as with the four-pound Strobonar V. (Some units have a half power switch and provide more flashes per battery.) When the Strobonar indicator lamp reaches a delay of 10 seconds and the Mighty Light DeLuxe 7 seconds, it's time for a battery change. The Strobonar V gives about one-half the intensity of a No. 5 bulb shot with the shutter at 1/200; the Mighty Light DeLuxe about one-quarter. The 60 w/s unit is the smallest that should be used. In the 60 to 100 w/s field there are many brands from which to choose. With film the speed of Tri-X, the light output of the Mighty Light DeLuxe is adequate to cover all wedding shots. In point of fact, the average altar shot (about 20 to 25 feet) can be taken at f/5.6, a cake shot (about 10 ft.) at f/12 when using a Mighty Light DeLuxe unit, a 4x5 camera, Royal Pan film and DK-50 developer. The depth of field in either shot is ample.

The third unit, the rechargeable wet-cell Ultra blitz Matador I is a veritable (135 w/s) powerhouse all packed into a 5-pound load. Its salient features: at full power an output greater than that of a No. 5 bulb with shutter at 1/200; window to show charge left in battery; can be operated off line electric current (ideal for studio use—also takes extension). I've gotten 30 full power and 75 half-power flashes from one charge without draining the battery. I have two Matador I units as I frequently shoot two weddings in one day.

About *Rechargeable Batteries*

For all practical purposes there arc only two basic types of rechargeable batteries readily available in the United States today. They are the wet-cell and nickel-cadmium batteries. You can recharge these batteries often and over a long period of time (but if not used for two weeks or so, they require short recharging).

Penny for penny, and watt-second input for watt-second input, the rechargeable cells mentioned have it all over the expendable dry-cell battery in candid wedding photography. Flashes cost next to nothing. And recharging is done by household (AC) current. I find I can easily cover one entire candid wedding before recharging. As a man in the business of candids I prefer the rechargeable battery.

Testing Flash and Electronic Flash Synchronization

Checking your shutter for synchronization is easy with electronic flash. Set your shutter at its highest speed (needed with electronic flash and synchro-sunlight) and your diaphragm wide open. Flash your unit about a foot in front of your lens. If you see a round disk on the ground glass, or on your lens through the open back of your camera, you are on the button. If you see the leaves of your shutter or no light at all your sync is off.

This test can be applied to the flashbulb but only as a rough check. If we were testing a shutter at 1/400 of a second, the No. 5 bulb's duration

31. *An intimate close-up may be made at smaller ceremonies such as this one (upper left), presided over by a fudge. (Busch Pressman; Tri-X; 60 tv/s electronic flash, 1/200, f/8; -film developed in DK-50.)* 32. *Another important picture in the church ceremony is when the couple turns to leave the altar (upper right). This is the only shot with altar as a background in which the bridal couple's faces show. Ordinarily, I shoot just after the couple has turned, trying to catch the maid of honor as she adjusts the train. Here, 1 saw that the bridal party formed a line on either side of the aisle so I adjusted focus and f/stop for 15 feet and waited until the couple reached the group before shooting. (Busch Pressman; Tri-X; No. 5 bulb, 1/200, f/14; DK-50.)* 33. *If there is no kissing shot at the altar, stop the couple at about the fifth pew from the end of the aisle. Ask them to kiss. The background will go nearly black but will establish the locale and couples rarely object to this dark background which imparts a sense of privacy. An alternate shot would catch the couple at about the third pew from the front so the parents and relatives would also be included. In the Protestant service, where the couple usually kisses before turning to walk down the aisle, this action may he caught then or re-enacted afterwards. (Konica III; Plus-X; 60 w/s electronic flash unit, 1/200 second, f/5.6; film developed in Microdol.)*

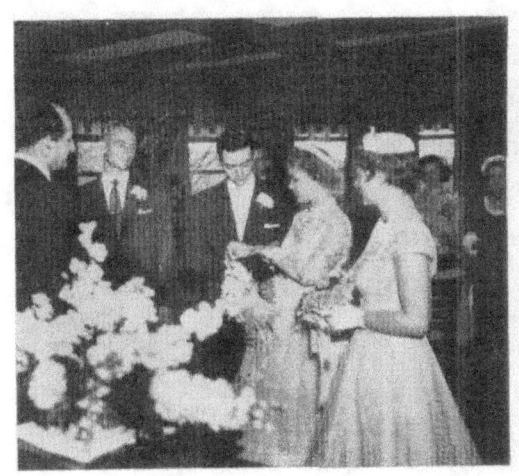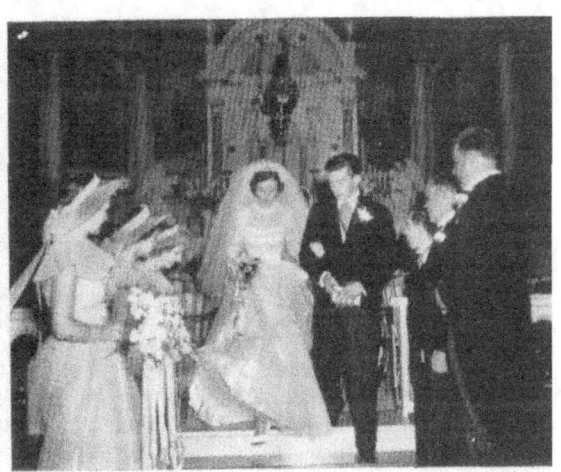

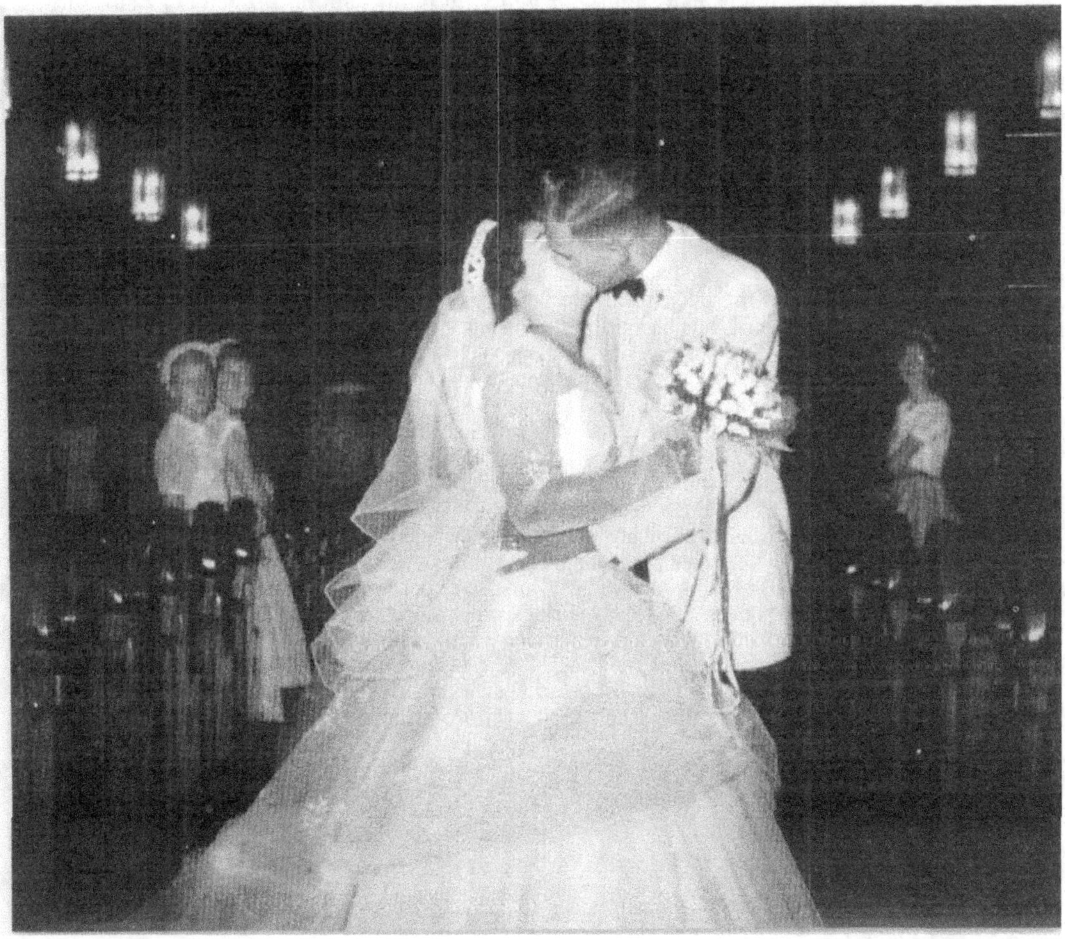

would be seven or eight times as long as the shutter's. The light we see would not necessarily be the peak of the flash. There are several homemade methods, as well as the Ansco Synchroflash Tester for detecting inaccurate flashbulb synchronization.

Synchronization and Press Cameras

In almost all cases, today's press camera shutters have an X setting for electronic flash, and an M setting for Class M flashbulbs. Work on any MX shutter can be done only by a skilled mechanic. Some press cameras have only X-sync, and a solenoid is used to synchronize Class M flashbulbs and the front shutter. Restoring this solenoid synchronization is rather involved and entails the loss of considerable time and the use of several flashbulbs. It is well worth the repairman's charge of about $2.

Testing Solenoid-Flashbulb Synchronization

If "sending the camera out" means a week or two, you can check the accuracy and adjust the shutter with this method:

On roll film cameras, place a piece of printing paper across the film plane and close the camera. Put your gun with bulb (without reflector) as close to the lens as you can accurately focus on it. Set the diaphragm wide open and the shutter at 1/200. Shoot. Develop the paper for about two minutes. With a press camera do the same but insert the paper in a holder.

If the bulb is *all* black, synchronization is on the button. If it is gray in the center and black toward the edges, shutter is late in opening. Turn solenoid screw down. If bulb is black in the center and grey toward the edges, the shutter is opening too soon. Turn the solenoid screw up. As I mentioned earlier, it's a lot of trouble for two dollars. This test can be made on internally synchronized shutters, but adjustment on them *must* be made only by a skilled camera repairman.

Should the occasion arise when you know your shutter is firing but you doubt its being on the button, shoot at 1/25 until you can change cameras or have the timing corrected.

Reciprocity Failure

"Reciprocity-law failure" is the incompatible partner of electronic flash. Understanding how it works (or doesn't) will explain all this talk of overdeveloping electronic flash negatives.

According to the "law of reciprocity," film that is exposed to "X" amount of light at a very fast shutter speed will have the same density (all other factors being equal) as the same kind of film also exposed to "X" amount of light, *but* at a very slow shutter speed. This does not hold true. A negative with a 1/10,000 second exposure will not be as dense as with 1/100 second exposure. This phenomenon is called reciprocity law failure, that is, the inability of film to respond normally to very short intense exposures, or at the other extreme, very long weak exposures. Reciprocity failure affects some films less than others. By developing the negative longer than the times recommended in the manufacturer's data sheet, for sunlight or flashbulb, we are able to compensate for this failure and attain both the density and contrast needed for printing on a No. 2 paper. With units of not too short a flash duration (1/500), little or no overdevelopment is needed.

Still the electronic flash manufacturers will recommend as much as 50 percent overdevelopment of film for general photography. I find that today's portable units of 1/1000 or 1/2000 second duration necessitate only a 10 percent overdevelopment. Longer developing will not increase the output of your unit—just the contrast of your film. The 50 percent overdevelopment applies to studio units of 1/10,000 second, or shorter, durations and is needed as these units are well within the range of reciprocity-law failure.

Guide Numbers and Electronic Flash

I use no guide number. Through repeated use you too will come to know the f/stop for every shot. Until then, the following data will be helpful to the photographer with limited experience.

In the table that follows, the lower guide numbers provide a half-stop more negative density than the higher ones. Your tests will give you an exact guide number somewhere between these limits, which will provide you with a safety factor of 2 for your individual unit.

FILM	STROBE	DEVELOPER	GUIDE NUMBER °	
Tri-X Film Pack	Ultra blitz Matador I (135 w/s)	DK-50	220 to 270	
or	Ultra blitz Matador I (½ power)	"	160	190
Royal Pan Cut Film	Strobonar V (80 w/s)	"	160	190
	Mighty Light DeLuxe (60 w/s)	"	110	135
Tri-X Roll Film	Ultra blitz Matador I	Microdol°°	190	220
	Ultra blitz Matador I (½)	"	135	160
	Strobonar V	"	135	160
	Mighty Light DeLuxe	"	95	110
Plus-X or Verichrome Pan	Ultra blitz Matador I	Microdol °°	120	145
	Ultra blitz Matador I (½)	"	84	100
	Strobonar V	"	84	100
	Mighty Light DeLuxe	"	60	70
Panatomic-X	Ultra blitz Matador I (smaller than 100 w/s not recommended)	D-76	75	90

° Up to one-half of the battery's potential number of flashes; beyond that, open ½-stop or decrease guide number 15 percent.

°°With D-76, close ½-1 stop or increase guide numbers by 20 percent. For candid weddings with 120/620 Tri-X, I prefer Microdol; with Verichrome Pan, D-76, with Plus-X or Tri-X 35mm, Microdol.

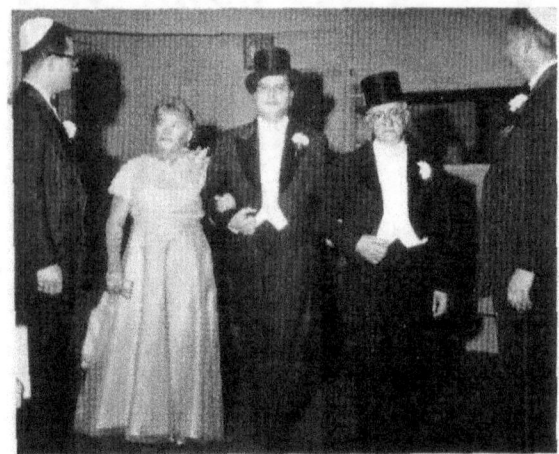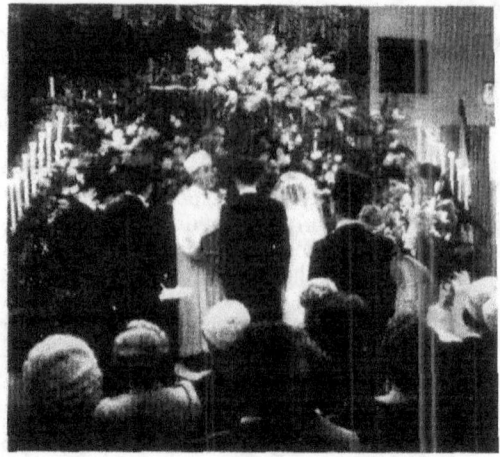

34. In the Jewish service the groom's parents escort him to the altar. (Mamiya 6; Tri-X; 60 w/s electronic flash, 1/200, f/7; Microdol.) 35. The shot at right is an available light shot made during the Jewish service. (Nikon, 35mm Nikkor lens; Tri-X; 1/30, f/1.8; FR X-500, diluted 1:10.)

Now for Some Pros and Cons

A good 60- to 135-watt second input electronic flash for professional use, means the initial outlay of about $70 to $125. The high voltage dry-cell batteries list for about $15, and regardless of how little they are used they have shelf life limits from about 6 to 12 months. There is also the hidden cost of repairs and the possibility of forgetting to turn off the power and burning out the batteries. (No, it hasn't happened to me yet, but as sure as tomorrow is another day, it will.)

The rechargeable-cell units, other than for the periodic battery charges, are no more trouble in actual operation than non-chargeable dry-cell units. But on the credit side is the $1.25 to $2.00 saved on each wedding by a rechargeable battery. The nickel-cadmium rechargeable-cell unit with its generous number of flashes per charge, should in time become the most popular choice with professionals. It should replace the less capable wet-cell and, unless dry-cell prices drop considerably, the high-voltage dry-cell unit as well.

With units powered by inexpensive "D" cells, shelf life is unimportant, but these units have in common a disturbing characteristic: recycling time for a full charge usually takes from 10 to 25 seconds. This delay is too long for candid weddings, and can mean the loss of important shots.

About Flashbulbs

For the man who shoots only an occasional wedding, the economical choice should be the flashbulb. The No. 5 or 25 (used with M-sync) is perfect for candids and 15 bulbs can fit comfortably into a man's coat pocket: enough for all the shots in church. {The No. 5 and 25 at 1/200, are roughly twice as powerful as an 80 w/s electronic flash unit or about equal to a 100 w/s unit.) With a flashbulb you know, to the penny, the cost of each flash. The price of a good BC (battery-capacitor) unit is from $5 to $15, and the batteries will last for as long as two years. Mechanical trouble with a BC unit is rare and failure of bulb to fire minimized. There isn't the added burden of carrying an electronic flash battery-pack. Camera motion should present no problem to the careful photographer, and most subject motion in a candid wedding picture can be stopped at 1/200 second.

This following chart gives the guide numbers for flash bulbs most commonly used in candid wedding photography, as well as the suitable film-developer combinations and shutter speeds.

FLASHBULB AT 1/200 SECOND

FILM	DEVELOPER	GUIDE NUMBER No. 5 or 25 Flashbulbs	No. 8 Flashbulb	FOCAL-PLANE SHUTTER SPEED	GUIDE NUMBER No. 6 or 26 Flashbulbs
Tri-X Film Pack	DK-50	210	185		
Royal Pan Cut Film	DK-50	210	185		
Tri-X Roll Film	Microdol °	180	150	1/100	180
				1/250	110
Verichrome Pan (Roll and Film Pack)	Microdol°	120	100	1/100	100
Plus-X (35mm)	Microdol °	120	100	1/100	100
Panatomic-X (1/100)	D-76	100		1/100	75

° With D-76 (undiluted) close diaphragm ½-1 f/stop, or increase guide number by 20 percent.

Note: At 1/200 second the No. 8 bulb has a guide number of one-third f/stop less than for the No. 5 but at 1/100 or slower it loses a full stop. At any shutter speed it is powerful enough with straight flash for Tri-X or Verichrome Pan or Plus-X. Of course, not enough can be said for its "peanut size" and some photographers may decide to stock both sizes using the No. 8 for church and reception and the No. 5 (with its greater output at 1/100 and 1/50) for partial bounce and very long shots. The No. 8 bulb is one cent per bulb cheaper.

Shutter inaccuracies do affect flash but not electronic flash guide numbers. Tests of your camera's speeds can be made by shooting a flashbulb exposure at the recommended guide number on color film for each shutter speed over 1/25 second and comparing them with one made with open flash. Kodachrome is the most suitable material for this test because of the exacting laboratory conditions under which it is processed. However, cheaper and more conclusive results can be gotten from a competent repairman. For about three dollars, he'll tell you, within 5 percent, the actual speed of each shutter setting. Remember, you'll avoid repairs and prolong the accuracy of your press camera shutter if—between jobs—you get into the habit of releasing the shutter and setting the speed at a setting under 1/100. With cameras that permit double exposures, cover the lens, trip your shutter then set speed under 1/100,

To Sum It All Up

The candid photographer who shoots a wedding every week or two will find the electronic flash a profitable investment that in time will pay off for itself. On the other hand, the not too active photographer may discover after "the thrill is gone," that contrary to what he has led himself to believe the electronic flash can be an expensive "economy." He will discover also, that though both flashbulb and electronic flash offer some individual benefits, the end results are practically the same; that if 1/1000 or 1/2000 second exposures intrigue him, flashbulb exposures of 1/400 or 1/500 (the speed of some electronic units) are not exactly a turtle's speed; that it is more trouble to carry a battery pack than a pocket full of bulbs; that changing bulbs takes little more time than switching a unit on or off.

From a practical standpoint, the decision to change from bulbs to electronic flash should be based only on a savings of dollars and cents. As time goes on the decision in favor of electronic flash will become progressively easier to make. Today there are, conservatively, twenty-five manufacturers of electronic-flash waging a war for supremacy. The result has been, and will continue to be, better units at cheaper prices.

36. *This picture is the equivalent of the shot made from the floor of the aisle during the Catholic ceremony. In this Jewish ceremony 1 shot by available light for a more interesting pictorial result. Using a Mamiya 6 camera and Tri-X film, I exposed a full second at f/5.6, developed in Microdol.*

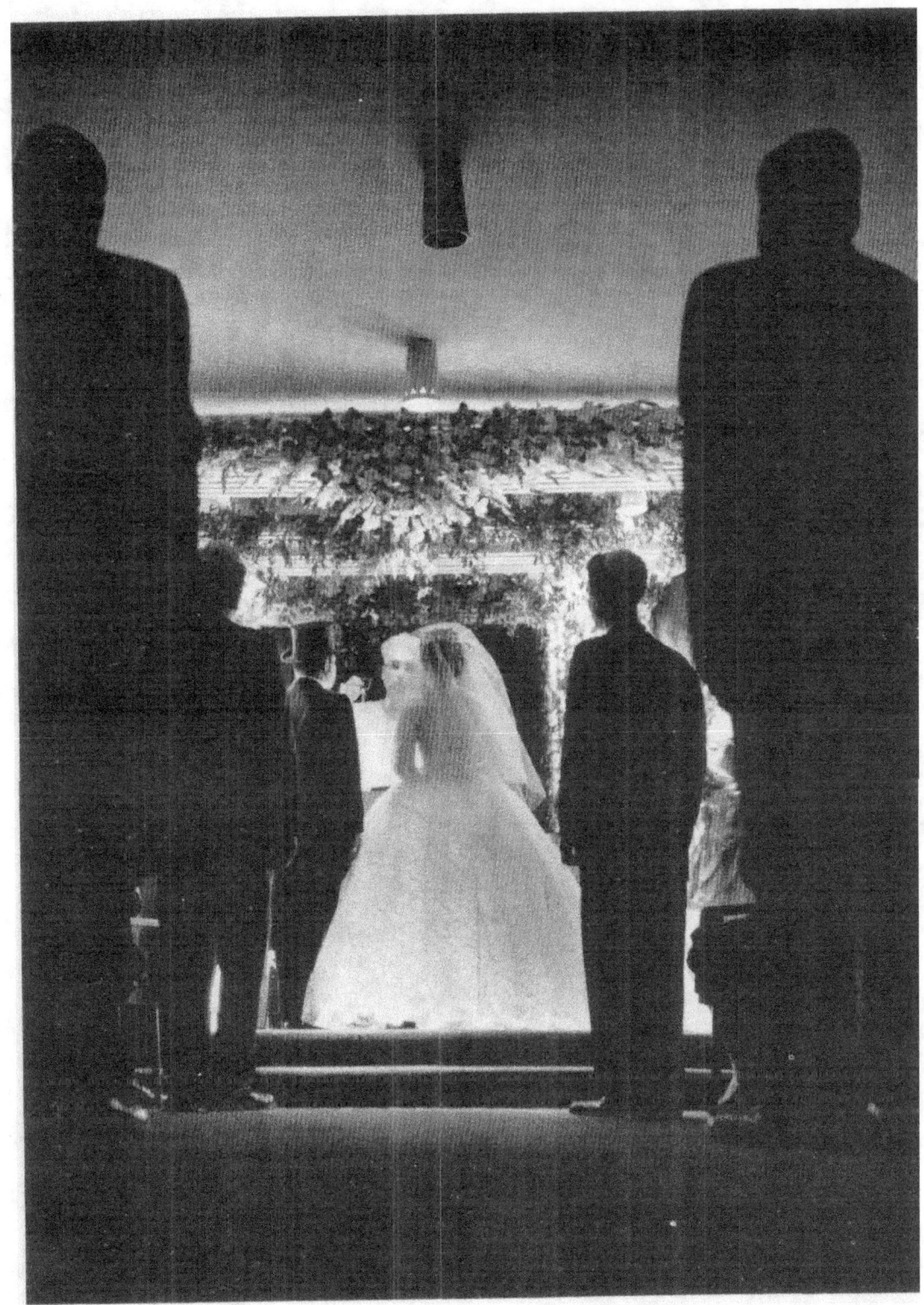

To conclude this summation there should be specific answers to the questions plaguing the photographer about to invest in his first electronic flash unit.

1. Dry-cell, wet-cell, nickel-cadmium battery, or "D" (flash-battery) cell? This question has been answered by the preceding paragraphs, but in em phasis it might be added the "D"-cell (flash-battery units) will not take the beating of candid shooting.

2. 60-80-100 watt second input? The 60 w/s will do with the fastest films, but partial bounce (see illustration 2) may be very limited (f/3.5 to f/4.5 with Tri-X at 12 ft.). The 80 w/s is a good compromise insofar as carrying weight and output are concerned. It will give satisfactory coverage with partial bounce (Tri-X, f/5.6 at 12 ft.). The 100 to 135 w/s, preferably with a ½ power switch, is ideal if most house shots are partial bounce. Full power can be used for partial bounce and 1/2 power for straight flash. I use the 135 w/s Ultra blitz Matador I at full power (partial bounce, f/5.6 at 12 ft. with Verichrome Pan and D-76 or Microdol; f/8 with Tri-X and Microdol).

5.

Synchro-Sunlight Photography

THE ABILITY TO SHOOT synchro-sunlight pictures is as important in candid weddings as the ability to shoot indoor flash. In this spread-out country of ours with its multitude of climates, outdoor photos can be taken from five to twelve months a year. But sunlight alone creates harsh facial shadows. Out of our bag of photographic tricks we pull flash and lighten these shadows. With this mating of sunlight and flash a new light is created—synchro-sunlight. In recent years, synchro-sunlight photography has become so popular in candid wedding photography that if the weather permits, the bridal couple takes it for granted that formals will be shot in an outdoor setting.

Of all the shots taken during the course of a candid, formals are the most critically scrutinized. For this reason synchro-sunlight exposures must be reasonably accurate, and not a hit-and-run, snapshot proposition.

With indoor flash all that is needed is a guide number for a particular film and flash combination. But, synchro-sunlight photography introduces another factor to consider—sunlight. Sunlight creates some minor problems, but these are more than balanced by the good it provides—another light source. With sunlight added, photographs sparkle, have modeling, and they do not have the flatness associated with straight flash!

"Glamour Lighting" with its heavy shadows should be avoided in wedding formals. A sunlight-flash ratio from about 2-to-l up to 4-to-l will provide a softness of lighting more in keeping with the bridal mood.

The candid wedding photographer has to work quickly. He hasn't got the time to fuss with exposure while the bridal couple or members of the bridal party wait patiently. He needs to have his exposures down pat for a wide variety of wedding situations, and synchro-sunlight is no exception. To help you achieve the same professional skill, here are some practical rules and short-cuts. But first, we must look at the basics: how to determine the exposure for sun without a meter; the flash guide number; and the fill-in ratio, or balance between sun and flash illumination.

Before establishing rules for synchro-sunlight let us first lay the foundation upon which these rules can be based:

49

.37. *Sometimes there is a reception line for the guests at the church. After focusing, watch the action for a moment when the faces of both bride and groom are not hidden by those of the guests. (Rolleiffex; Tri-X; 80 w/s electronic flash, 1/250, f/7; film developed in Microdol.)* 38. It *is desirable to have a shot which includes the clergyman and the couple. An opportunity for this may occur in the vestibule following the service. You can pose the clergyman as he hands the marriage certificate to the groom or shakes his hand, or all three may look directly at the camera. If there is no opportunity at the church you may get this picture later at the reception. (Konica III; Plus-X; 80 w/s electronic flash unit, 1/200, f/8; Microdol.)*

39. *The best results with a shot such as this will be obtained if you issue instructions immediately beforehand. To be sure that at the last moment no one steps between you and the couple, ask them to hesitate at the door of the church until you beckon and then to advance, ignoring the camera. Ask several people to throw their rice or confetti when the couple reaches a designated spot or step. Catching the rice in mid-air will make this appear to be a truly "candid" shot. The candid wedding photographer should not hope for a good shot—he should set it up ahead of time. Pre-focus for about 15 feet. A frequent fault is catching the couple when they are too close to the camera. (Busch Pressman; Tri-X; No. 5 bulb, 1/200, f/14; film developed in DK-50.)*

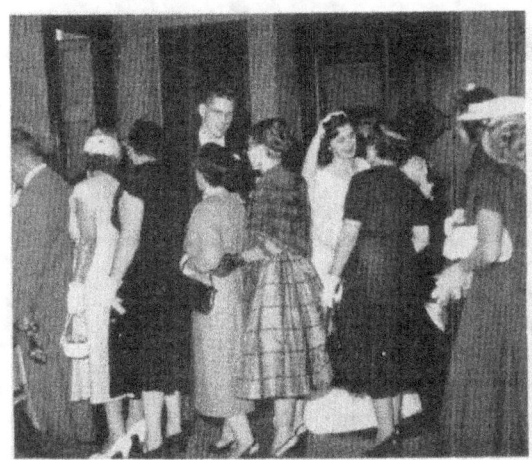
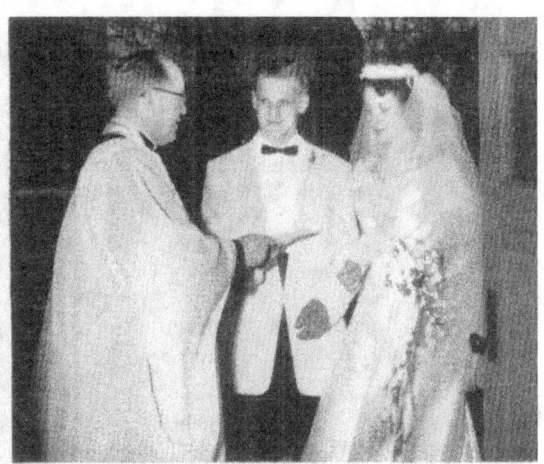

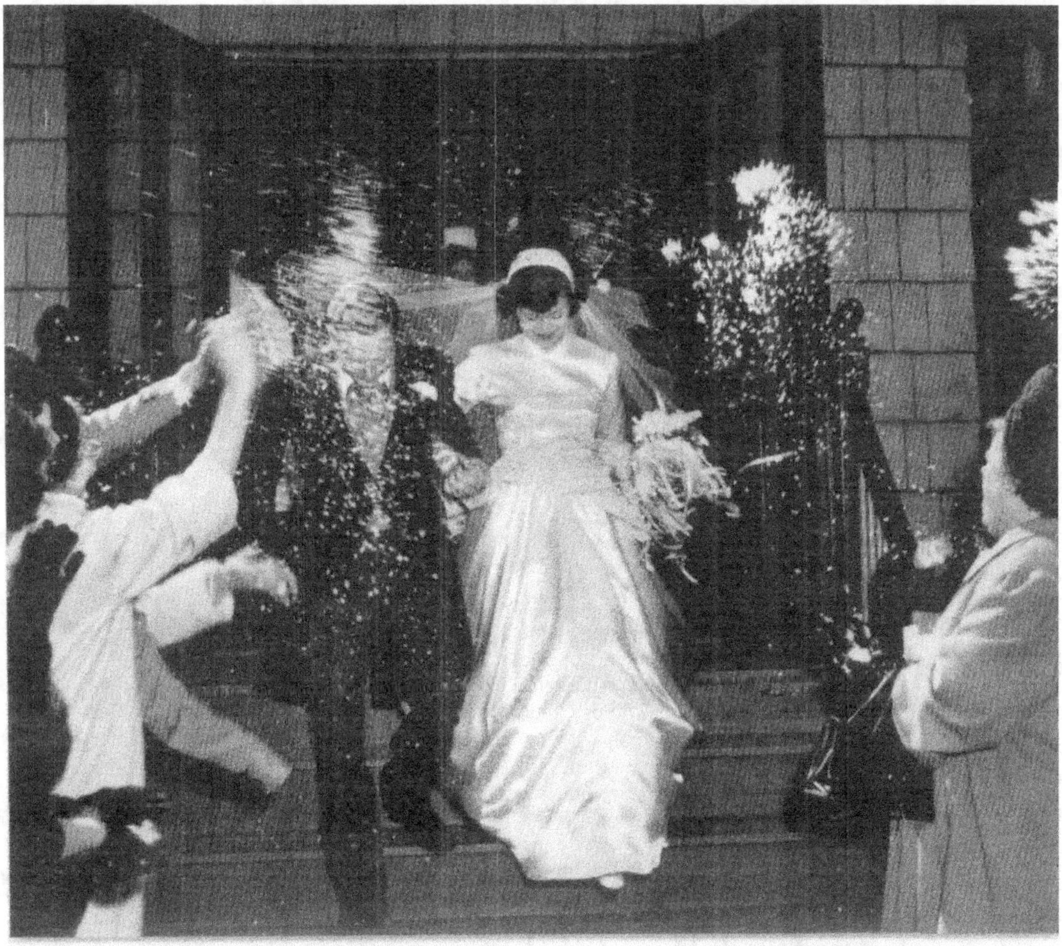

1. No light meter is needed for synchro-sunlight on a clear, sunny day when the sun is facing the subject. Just place the number "1" over the ex posure index rating (film speed). This fraction is the basic shutter speed for f/16 with *any* film developed in fine-grain developer. This is also the shutter speed for f/19 (halfway between f/16 and f/22) and *any* film developed in active developers such as DK-60a, D-76, or DK-50. Suppose you're using Tri-X film developed in Microdol? By placing "1" over the 200 film speed, you arrive at an exposure of 1/200 at f/16. If you are shooting with Royal Pan (devel oped in DK-50), again you'd place "1" over the film speed of 200. But this time you'd have an exposure of 1/200 at f/19.

2. For simplicity's sake we've settled on just a few guide numbers. With No. 5 and 52 flashbulbs and 1/200 second, we use the flashbulb guide num ber of 180 suggested by Eastman Kodak for Tri-X film developed in Microdol. However, film exposed by flashbulb and developed in active developers such as DK-60a, D-76, or DK-50 is about half a stop faster than film processed in a fine-grain developer. So for all Tri-X film and Royal Pan sheet film (with No. 5 or 25 bulb and 1/200 shutter speed), we used the guide number of 210 if the film is to be developed in one of these more active developers. Guide num bers for other films are given in the chart in Chapter 4 (Flash and Electronic Flash).

3. It is important to remember that the above sunlight and flashbulb guides allow for a black-and-white safety factor of 2—that is, one f/stop over-exposure (actually this is a safety factor of *2Vz,* which is 1¼ f/stops. See No. 5 below).

4. Providing a guide number for each of the many electronic flash units would not be of lasting benefit. Almost weekly, new models are introduced and older models are either improved or discontinued. Manufacturer's guide numbers generally are more optimistic than factual, and the photographer will do well to establish his own guide numbers for his specific unit. (See Chapter 4.) In examples that follow, I will use the popular 80 watt-second input, Stro-bonar V for exploring the possibilities of electronic flash for synchro-sunlight photography.

5. Synchro-sunlight wedding photos are not examined with professional scrutiny as far as fill-in ratios are concerned. They should be close but there is no need for exactness. As I said before, bridal parties often get impatient. The candid wedding photographer is not always afforded the luxury of leisureliness.

Two Rules for Synchro-Sunlight

So we need a rule or two—which can be applied quickly—in fact more quickly than it takes to tell you about them. *One rule* for fill-in applies to all situations where flashbulbs are used—with between-the-lens, behind-the-lens, or focal-plane shutters (and FP flashbulbs). This rule also applies to elec-tronic flash when speeds of 1/25 or 1/50 are the fastest you can use due to shutter construction. Focal plane shutters fall into this category. {A second rule is needed for use of electronic flash with a camera having full—all speed— X synchronization. But more on that, and what to do, later).

Using the First Rule

First: As outlined before, determine the shutter speed for bright sun by placing 1 over the exposure index number (film speed) given in the manufacturer's instruction sheet. Then if the film is fine-grain developed set the diaphragm at f/16; if a more active developer is used, f/19.

Now: Divide the f/stop into your flashbulb or electronic flash guide number. The answer is the number of feet from subject to fill-in light.

Offhand it might appear that this rule gives a 1-to-1 ratio but, remember, the guide numbers recommended in the table for electronic flash (Ultra blitz Matador I, Heiland V and Mighty Light DeLuxe), as well as the flashbulb guide numbers have a safety factor of one f/stop. This is nullified by the loss of one f/stop in effectiveness when flash is used outdoors. Does this loss also occur in large indoor areas such as church and reception halls? Yes, but the over-development needed to build up contrast preserves the safety factor. With synchro-sunlight, there is no overdevelopment. We are left with a fill-in of normal intensity and a one f/stop overexposure by sun for a 2-to-1 rati

Note: Once the shutter settings and fill-in distance are established, moving the light 30 percent closer to the subject doubles the light intensity; moving 50 percent away cuts it in half. To illustrate this graphically, substitute feet for the f/ on the numbers of the lens openings.

from one distance to the next doubles flash intensity

←————————————————————————

FEET: 5.6   8   11   16   22   32

from one distance to the next cuts flash intensity in half

————————————————————————→

The photographer can set his camera quickly with this system. It's easy to memorize a basic bright sun exposure such as 1/200 and f/16 or 19. It's equally easy to figure out the basic fill-in distance, ahead of time, by dividing f/16 or 19 into your guide number. Now let's test the one rule (and later the exception) to see how we can vary the fill-in distance easily.

The First Rule, and How to Apply It

The film is Royal Pan (Daylight-200); developer, DK-50; flash, No. 5 bulb (guide number 210). Our basic exposure is 1/200 (or 1/250), and f/19. 210 -f- 19 = an 11-foot fill-in distance—ideal for shots of bride, bride and groom and small groups taken 12 to 13 feet from the subjects.

For larger groups (about 15 ft.) either leave the gun on the camera for a 4:1 ratio or for a brighter fill-in use an extension cord and place the gun at 13 instead of 11 feet to make sure the people at the outer ends of the picture are covered. I would leave the gun on the camera.

For eight foot shots, again the reflector on extension cord can be left at 11 feet, but be certain that the fill-in is higher and a little to one side of your head in order to avoid including your own shadow (by flash) in the picture area. *Or,* leave the gun on the camera and for a 2:1 ratio use one thickness of white handkerchief over the reflector.   *Or,* use a No. 8 bulb. The handker-

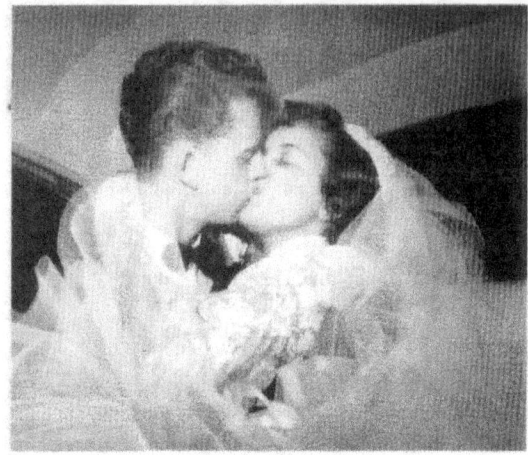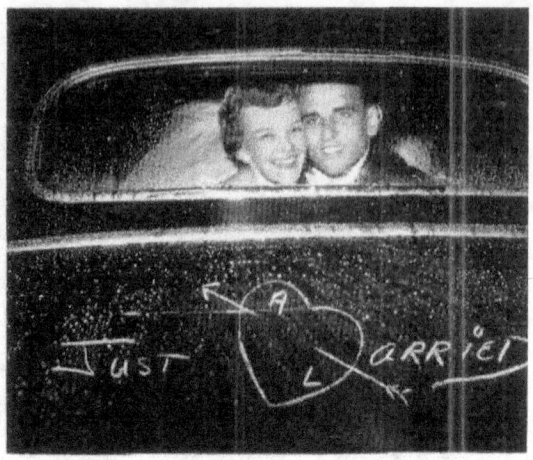

40. The kiss in the car should be posed. Tell the couple not to kiss hard enough to distort their features. (Rolleiflex; Tri-X; 80 w/s electronic flash, 1/250, f/22; Microdol.) 41. Shooting through the rear window, ask them to smile, check-to-cheek. The "just married" sign was made by writing on the printing paper with a soft pencil before exposure. (Data as above, except f/14.)

chief is less trouble and dispenses with the need for stocking No. 8 bulbs, or for use of extension.

The No. 5 bulb is ideal for synchro-sunlight formals. Without removing the gun from your camera, it will give close to a 4:1 ratio at 15 feet; 2:1 at 11 feet; and (with one layer of white handkerchief) 2:1 at 8 feet with *any black-and-white film* shot at 1/100 or higher.

The Second Rule

If you have a fully synchronized X shutter and are using electronic flash you must apply another rule for synchro-sunlight photography. These shutters are of the between-the-lens and behind-the-lens types, and one is similar to the other. The behind-the-lens shutter, is as the words say, located behind the shutter to permit lens interchangeability and provides greater flash freedom than is possible with a focal plane shutter. But all information provided here for the between-the-lens shutter can be applied directly to the behind-the-lens shutter.

An electronic flash unit of 80 to 100 or more watt-seconds input and a between-the-lens fully synchronized X shutter form an especially compatible combination for synchro-sunlight photography.

Whether the camera shutter speed is 1 second or 1/800 second, the film receives the same amount of light from an electronic flash unit of 1/1000 second or shorter (faster) duration.

The rule for synchro-sunlight with electronic flash and the fully synchronized X shutter is a contradiction to the flashbulb rule of determining the daylight exposure first, then computing the fill-in distance. Instead: divide the number of feet from the electronic flashtube to subject into the electronic flash guide number to determine the f/stop (the same as for indoor shots). Then: use the shutter speed that is needed in sunlight for this f/stop.

Let's Try Out the Second Rule

All material is the same as for the flashbulb fill-in example but this time the Heiland V is substituted for the No. 5 bulb and the camera shutter must be *fully* X synchronized. (This rule cannot be applied to an X shutter limited to 1/25 or 1/50 synchronization.)

Suppose distance from subject to camera, with electronic flash attached is 12 feet? We apply the first step of our rule by dividing 12 into 160 (the guide number of our unit). The answer is f/13⅓ (halfway between f/11 and f/16). Now we establish the exposure for sunlight. The exposure rating for Royal Pan outdoors is 200. We place the number "1" over 200 and find that the basic camera setting for bright sunny days is 1/200 at f/19 (halfway between f/16 and f/22). To shoot at f/13½ we merely change the shutter speed from 1/200 to 1/400 for a 2:1 fill-in ratio.

With a 15 foot shot, the same electronic flash calls for almost f/11. With a 1/500 and 1/400 shutter the ratios will be 2:1 and 3:1 respectively. For an 8 foot shot, 160 ÷8 = 20, so use an exposure of 1/200 and f/20.

From bridal party group (15 feet) down to a three-quarter length shot (7-8 feet) we have not had to remove the light from the camera, have had to use no handkerchief or extension. All this was done with a light having one half the intensity of a No. 5 bulb shot at 1/200!

The results with a 60-watt second electronic flash unit (guide number 120) are almost as flexible. Such a unit is comparable in light output to a Westinghouse M-2 flashbulb used at 1/100. For the examples below the gun was on the camera.

At 15 feet: 120 ÷15 =* f/8. Use 1/800 (only the Kodak Rapid Synchro 800 Shutter has this speed setting) for a 3:1 ratio; 1/500 for 4:1; 1/400 for 5:1 (5:1 is still a pleasant ratio).

At 12 feet: 120 ÷ 12 = almost f/11. Use 1/500 for a 2:1, 1/400 for 3:1.

At 8 feet: 120 ÷ 8 = almost f/16. Use 1/200 (1/250) for 3:1.

Synchro-Sunlight and the Focal-Plane Shutter

The focal-plane shutter can be avoided in the press cameras, but it is the shutter most often found in the expensive 35mm. In practice, at the speeds normally employed in candid wedding work, the focal plane shutter is more accurate than other shutters. With Class M bulbs it is not so practical as the between-the-lens fully synchronized MX shutter. And it is just about useless with electronic flash for synchro-sunlight.

The slow shutter speeds of 1/25 to 1/50 necessary for electronic flash synchronization with focal plane shutters, result in closed-down f/stops for sunlight. It is these small f/stops that impose the crippling limitations on the popular 60- to 100-watt-second units.

The first synchro-sunlight rule (see page 53) applies, *but* . . . . if you're shooting with medium speed or high speed films you'll need a filter (medium yellow or neutral density) to bring the f/stop down to the f/16 or 22 you have from the f/32 you haven't got. And by the time you get through, all you will have for your trouble is the ineffectual fill-in distances of 3 to 5 feet for a 2:1 ratio.

Discouraging? Well, don't give up. This limitation applies only to synchro-sunlight photos. Now, let us try synchro-shade (in shade with open sky above).

Synchro-Shade

The camera in all probability, is a 35mm, so we will assume that the shutter is a focal-plane and the exposure is based on Plus-X (daylight 80), developed in Microdol. Basic exposure: **1/80,** f/16. Electronic flash: Strobonar V with a guide number of 96 for Plus-X. No filter.

The shutter speed must be confined to between 1/25 to 1/50 in order to synchronize with electronic flash. At 1/25, the f/stop for sun is roughly f/32, or for open shade f/11 (open 3 stops). Divide 11 into 96 and we have the now useable distance of almost 9 feet for a 2:1 ratio and about 13½ feet for a 4:1.

For the fifteen foot group shots leave the electronic flash gun on the camera. The fill-in ratio is not important as shadows in the shade are already soft. The 9 foot fill-in distance is less than 2:1 for the three-quarter length shots with the reflector on the camera. One thickness of handkerchief over the reflector will give a more pronounced modeling.

With the camera synchronized for 1/50 the situation is just about perfect. At 1/50 the f/stop for shade is roughly f/8. 96 ÷ 8 = 12 feet, a perfect 2:1 for 12 foot shots; a 3:1 for 15 feet and a 2:1 for 8 foot shots with a handkerchief over the reflector.

Of course, the slow shutter speeds (1/25 to 1/50) necessary for electronic flash synchronization can cause "ghost" or double images either by camera movement or subject motion. The film can register with a daylight image and another image from the lightning-like duration of the electronic flash. But a tripod will eliminate the possibility of camera movement and also facilitate handling the electronic flash, with an extension cord, away from the camera.

After making those synchro-shade pictures, try some shots without flash. Portraits taken in the shade arc soft and flattering: the subject's features are relaxed and devoid of squinting. Flash, though useful, is not so essential as with direct sunlight.

We used the Heiland Strobonar V in our synchro-shade example, but any electronic flash that is strong enough can be substituted simply by applying the guide numbers for that unit.

Synchro-Sun with Focal-Plane Flashbulbs

By changing to a focal-plane bulb the photographer using a focal-plane shutter is less restricted in synchro-sunlight photography than he is with electronic flash. This bulb differs from the M-type bulb in that the flash duration resembles a plateau rather than a mountain peak. The long, even, duration of light permits the use of many focal-plane shutter speeds by providing a uniform amount of light us the slit of the focal-plane shutter travels across the face of the film.

Deciding which focal-plane bulb to use is simple and depends on your negative size. Generally, the No. 6 and 26 bulbs are recommended, at a variety of speeds, for cameras making negatives from 35mm up to and including 21/4x31/4 (small Speed Graphic size). The No. 31 and 2A bulbs have a more extended plateau or peak, and are designed for use at a variety of speeds with the larger focal-plane shutter cameras. However the 31 and 2A can be used at reasonable efficiency with the smaller size negatives if you set your shutter at 1/25 second.

For specific examples, let's say we're shooting with the same 35mm camera used for synchro-shade on page 56. Again the camera is loaded with Plus-X (daylight rating 80) which will be developed in Microdol. For the first picture we will shoot by synchro-sunlight using a fast shutter speed and an FP 6 flashbulb. Our basic exposure for sunlight is 1/80 at f/16. We have no 1/80 so we will use 1/100, and compensate by opening the diaphragm to f/14 (a quarter stop under f/16). Next, the guide number for the FP 6 (or 26) bulb at 1/100 is 100. Then, we divide 100 by f/14 and arrive at a fill-in distance of 7 feet for a 2:1 ratio. Leaving the flashgun on the camera for the 10-11 foot shots will result in a 4:1 ratio.

Now let's see what happens if we take the same set-up—35mm focal-plane camera, Plus-X film and 1/100 shutter speed—but substitute an FP 31 flashbulb for the FP 6? The FP 31 at 1/100 will add nothing to the 7-foot fill-in distance despite its 77-81,000 lumen seconds output as compared with the 15-17,000 of an FP 6. At 1/100 most 35mm focal-plane cameras only use a portion of the light emitted by this bulb, with its greatly extended peak, or plateau. If you try 1/25 with an FP 31 or 2A in a 6- to 7-inch polished reflector you will have an improved fill-in because you will be using the light output more efficiently,

For the FP 31 with your 35mm focal-plane shutter camera you need a neutral density filter so that the smallest diaphragm opening on your lens (often f/16) can be used. The guide number for the FP 31 or 2A (with 4X neutral density filter, and Plus-X film developed in Microdol) is 160; 160 divided by f/16 = 10 feet. The ratio is 2:1. With an f/22 diaphragm, and a K2 filter, you can use a guide number of 220 for either the FP 31 or 2A. In this case 220 divided by f/22 still gives you a 10-foot fill-in distance. Whichever guide number you use, leaving the gun on the camera for the 12 to 13 foot shots will result in a 3:1 ratio, and for the 15 feet (larger group pictures), 4:1. Shooting with an FP 6 bulb at 1/100 is perfect for the 7 to 8 foot shots where you want a 2:1 ratio. So by using two kinds of focal plane flashbulbs with your 35mm focal plane camera, you can make most of your synchro-sunlight exposures without resorting to an extension cord.

Other Cases

What do you do if you have a 2¼x2¼ single-lens reflex camera with focal-plane shutter? Just follow instructions given for using the 35mm's focal-plane shutter. With press cameras, you have a synchronized front shutter, so the back focal-plane shutter is rarely used for flash of any sort. But, if your front shutter ever gives you trouble, and you have to resort to the focal-plane for flash, the same rules apply. However, the bigger bulbs (FP 31 or 2A) will give you better coverage than the FP 6 or 26, with press cameras larger than

Synchro-Sunlight and Special Effects

Backlighting: Beautiful effects can be created through backlighting (when the sun is behind your subject). The closer the camera gets to the subject the more dramatic the effect. For this reason the candid wedding photographer should concentrate his backlighting on the three-quarter length shots of bride alone, or bride and groom. With backlighting the flash now becomes the main light, as little or no sunlight reaches the front of the subject. To obtain the safety factor of 2, open up one f/stop more than for fill-in purposes. This will take care of both backlight (sun) and front light (flash).

Side lighting: Treat side lighting by sun the same as a normal synchro-sunlight exposure. Side lighting is not recommended on more than one person —shadows will be thrown from one onto the other. A lens-shade must be used with either side or backlight.

Open Shade: Open shade means in the shadow of an object such as a tree, but with a blue sky above. For our purposes the open shade of a sunny day is constant and poses no problem. It calls for three f/stops more exposure than sunlight. Subjects under an object and receiving no direct skylight should be given four f/stops more than for sunlight. In either case, if no flash is used, develop film 30 percent more than for synchro-sunlight exposures.

Hazy Days: Hazy or overcast days need not prevent outdoor bridal photos. The lighting will be soft and the modeling good. Flash is not essential, but if desired, the rules already established for determining a fill-in distance still apply. If flash fill-in is used, determine the daylight exposure through the use of a meter. Unlike open shade, the light of cloudy days is not constant and can lead to a variety of exposures. Care must be taken never to have the flash stronger than the daylight as this will result in an unnatural night-like effect.

General Suggestions

Keep lighting simple with the bridal party or groups. Placing your subjects at an angle to the sun will minimize the tendency to frown or squint, but a sunlight angle of 45 degrees is the greatest angle that should be attempted.

The purpose of a fill-in light is to "open up" or lighten the shadow areas. The reflector, on extension cord, must be kept as close as possible to the line between subject and camera. This is so shadows on the subject's face do not conflict with those of the sun or any main light such as hazy sun, cloudy-bright or open shade.

Standardize your synchro-sunlight (or shade) shooting distances so that through repetition both shutter adjustment and placement of the fill-in light becomes automatic. These three distances will take care of all your "formals."

15 to 17 feet: groups of twelve to sixteen people. (See photo 47 of large group for placement of subjects.)

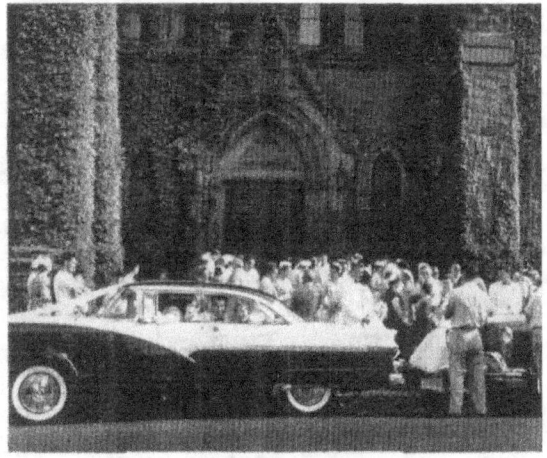

42. *From across the street toe can include the face of the church, the cars and the spectators for an atmosphere shot. Expose for daylight. (Minolta Autocord; Tri-X; 1/200, f/11.)*

12 to 13 feet: bride, bride and groom, and small groups up to six people.

7 to 8 feet: ¾ length shots of bride, or bride and groom. If composition closer than three-quarter length should be requested by the couple when they are selecting proofs, blowing up the three-quarter shot will do the trick with no possibility of distortion. Such a request is rare. The bride has gone to considerable trouble to get just the gown she wants and is not apt to ask for a head and shoulder photo that cuts off most of it.

The flash and electronic flash data can be affected by two variables-accuracy of shutter, and design or finish of reflector. A slightly inaccurate shutter—whether slow or fast—will not affect the electronic flash guide number, but the increased or decreased exposure by sun (or daylight) will alter the fill-in ratios. At normal shooting speeds, flashbulb synchro-sunlight ratios remain unaffected when the shutter speed is 1/100 or faster. But the inaccurate shutter will affect both the sun and flashbulb exposures and result in either a denser or thinner negative.

Flashbulb synchro-sunlight ratios can be affected when a speed of 1/50 is used and the shutter is slow. The flashbulb output at 1/50 or slower is the same as that of open flash. It has reached its maximum output. But a slow 1/50 shutter speed which in reality may be 1/25, will increase the synchro-sunlight ratio by creating more than calculated negative density by sun.

With a normal lens, a shallow reflector will be less efficient than a deeper one, because it spreads light over a wider angle than necessary. A highly polished surface will throw more light ½stop) than a satin finish. (Guide numbers are based on a polished reflector.)

There is another factor to be considered. A between-the-lens shutter's efficiency is calibrated at its largest opening. Today's sensitive films have created the need for higher shutter speeds and small lens openings particularly with synchro-sunlight shots. This combination can increase the shutter's efficiency to the point of a full stop overexposure. To get a thinner negative, reduce the exposure, or use your K-2, X-l, or 4X neutral density filter to get your aperture down to f/8 or f/11.

Fortunately, the latitude of black-and-white films used for candid is broad enough to absorb these tolerances. A shutter can be 100 percent inaccurate (usually slow) and the reflector any of a hundred makes and still the negative will be of sufficient quality to produce good prints—if we respect the ASA ratings and their safety factor of one and a quarter f/stops.

Filters and Synchro-Sun

Filters play no important roll in black-and-white candids except for outdoor shots. If trees or shrubbery are behind the subject no filter is essential. However, for the perfectionist, a light green (XI) filter will lighten the green background, darken slightly any portion of sky that can be seen and give the subjects a healthy-looking tan complexion (with pan films). The light yellow, and medium yellow filters (Kl or K2), can be used to darken the sky and bring out the clouds. With fast film used outdoors, neutral density filters (4X to 10X) permit you to open up your lens to, say, f/5.6 or f/4.5, or even f/2, in order to obtain desirable and less distracting out-of-focus backgrounds so pleasing to outdoor formals.

6.

4x5 Cameras

THE FAMILIAR 4x5 PRESS CAMEBA is used almost exclusively in shooting candid weddings. It is the candid photographer's badge. The 4x5 was passed down to us by the newspaper photographer who found it convenient to be able to shoot as little as one snot and to use a film size easy to handle and one that would show no objectionable grain with active developers.

The first internally synchronized shutters, X or MX, were designed for the camera most used for serious flash work—the 4x5 Press. Internally synchronized shutters did not appear on roll film cameras until about ten years later (1951); fully synchronized shutters about 1953. More than anything else, the G.I. Bill of Rights provided the impetus that was to establish the 4x5 as the camera for flash photography. To the many thousands of these students the schools recommended the 4x5 as the ideal "all around" camera! It was built for flash, the film was amply sized for portrait retouching and the controls flexible enough for most commercial assignments. Find a photography school student and you're likely to find a 4x5 camera. As candid weddings became increasingly popular, the studios and students found each other.

Four of the most used 4x5's are the Speed or Crown Graphic, Busch-Pressman, Linhof and the B&J Press. They are all bellows type. The Graphic is by far the most popular. Sheet film holders, film pack adapters and the six-film Grafmatic holder can be used in any 4x5 springback camera. This is important in case of camera breakdown.

Studios are adapted for handling 4x5 film and not many will hire a man with a smaller film size camera. The 4x5 provides a healthy margin of safety for the candid photographer who is timid about filling up his negatives.

Lenses *and Shutters*

The most popular focal length for the 4x5 press camera is the 135mm *(5Yi* inch). Its shorter than normal focal length makes it a desirable lens for working in close quarters, gives additional depth of field and provides ample coverage at f/stops used in flash work. The lenses commonly found on press cameras sold in this country are: the 135mm Wollensak Raptar, Graflex Optar, Schneider Xenar, and the (127mm) Kodak Ektar. All are coated, and all can

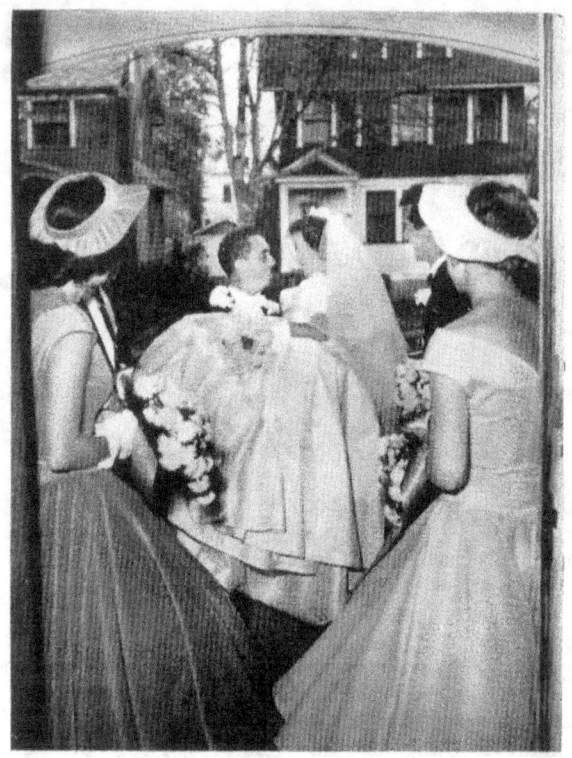

43. *This is, of course, a posed shot so any doorway will do either at the home or at the reception. Shooting from a high vantage point such as an inside stairway will make for more interesting perspective. (Rolleiflex; Tri-X; 80 w/s electronic flash, 1 /100, f/11; film developed in Microdol.)*

be had with MX, fully synchronized shutters. The lens is usually an f/4.5 or f/4.7 of four-element design. F/4.7 is fast enough, especially with today's high speed films.

A between-the-lens, fully synchronized, MX shutter eliminates the need for battery-draining solenoids. It permits an instant switch to flashgun or electronic flash if either unit should give trouble. A shutter speed range from one second to 1/200 is acceptable, but 1/400 or faster is preferable. The one second to 1/400 shutter almost always accompanies the press camera lens.

A solenoid activated shutter is not less expensive than an MX fully synchronized shutter. To the busy candid wedding photographer the MX shutter is preferable because the cost of battery changes can mean the price of a new lens and shutter every three to five years. On the other hand, the solenoid has two advantages. First, when a long extension cord is used, you can activate the shutter by means of a button on the flashgun. Second, if your work calls for simultaneous black-and-white and color exposures from the same flashbulb, with a Candid Stereo Bracket, you'll need a solenoid on one of the two cameras.

Otherwise, if the flashbulb is used within reach of your camera, and you have a substitute camera, and both cameras are MX synchronized, the solenoid is an accessory you'll never use.

The focal plane shutter on the Speed Graphic is a hazard that may spell *no pictures*. For electronic flash, this back shutter is not really useful because it can only be used at 1/25 second. Its advantage of rapid speed, on the other hand, is rarely useful to the wedding photographer who works at more normal shutter speeds. The sole advantage of the back shutter is that less-expensive barrel-mounted lenses of either wide-angle or longer than normal focal lengths may be employed.

Before getting off the subject of the 4x5 press camera I would like to comment on some long overdue improvements. The sheet film holder may answer the purpose of the newspaper or commercial photographer but it falls miserably short as fast and efficient equipment for the man who has 50 or more shots to take, often one right after the other. It takes four motions to put in the holder, pull out the slide, replace the slide and pull out the holder to take one picture. Multiply this by 50 and you have a lot of work just handling the film. With this, include the time and energy wasted in going to the carrying case after every four or six exposures. The Grafmatic, which holds six sheet films, is an improvement but still inadequate. You will need 10 Grafmatic holders, and as with the regular two-film holder, it's quite a job of loading. Larger holders styled on the discontinued 12 to 18 sheet film septums would add substantial weight to an already cumbersome camera. Film packs are perfect but, it costs $10 to $11 to shoot a candid wedding with them and that's a lot of money for film. What about a 4x5 roll film holder built on the order of the ones being used on the miniature press cameras that would hold about a 25-shot roll? Buckling of film? Why should it buckle anymore than in the six exposure 118 (3¼x4¼) or 122 (3¼x5½) roll film sizes? A single or multiple roll film developing tank should present no problem. Or as a second choice, a 25-shot film pack constructed the same as the present film pack would be a great help and would I am sure, cut production and packaging costs. Jamming? If it were as reliable as the present pack there would be no cause for complaint. I have used film packs for 10 years—used thousands—and not one has ever jammed.

To complete the circle of an accurate rangefinder, a sharp lens, a synchronized shutter, a remarkable flashbulb or the astounding electronic flash, we need a device for the press and roll film camera that would automatically adjust the f/stop for flashbulb or electronic flash as we focused. It would end the most persistent trouble in flash photography—bad exposures. The 35mm Bolsey Jubilee Set-O-Matic has such a provision.

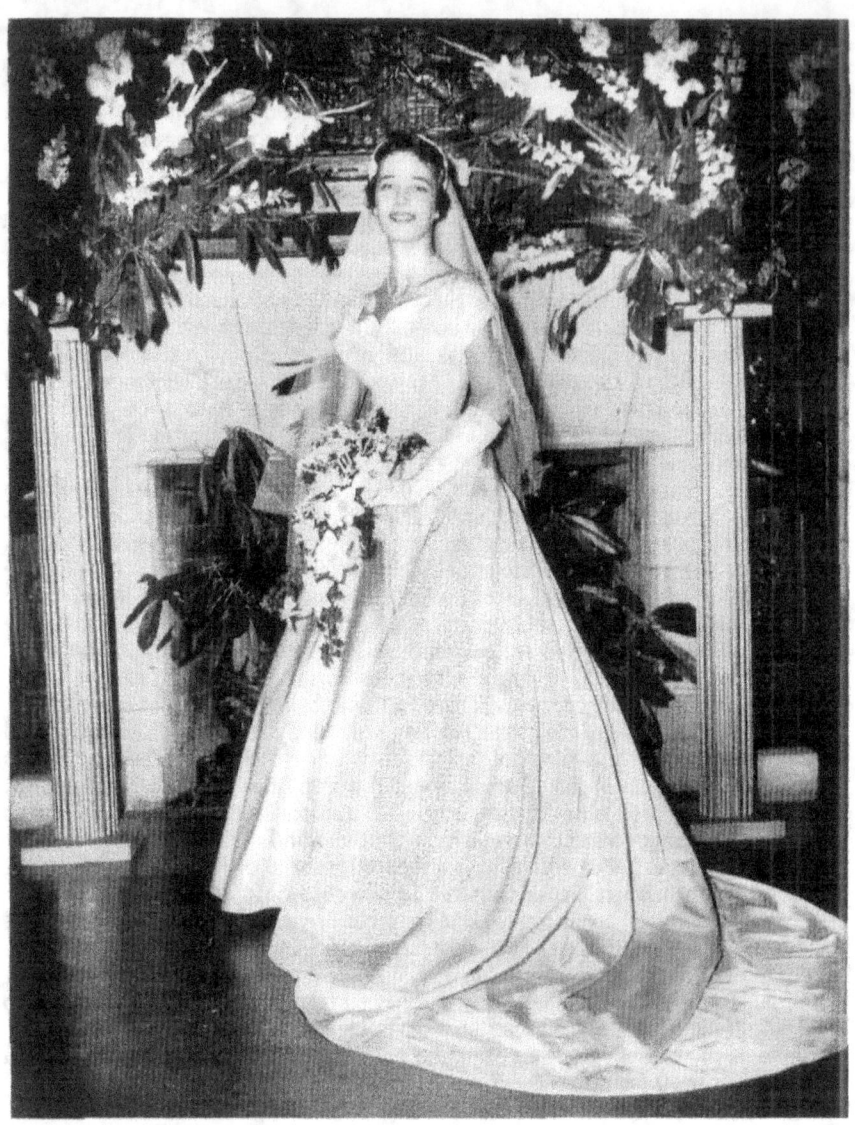

44. *If formals of the bride alone were not made at the house they can be made during the reception. They are generally made front face although the head may be turned slightly for a more -flattering angle, and the shoulders and hips should usually be turned to a three-quarter angle from the camera. The candid wedding photographer must usually work with only one light to achieve his effects. (Busch Pressman; Tri-X; 60 w/s electronic flash unit, 1/200 second, f/10; film was developed in DK-50.)*

7

Roll Film Cameras

IF THE WORDS "Candid Wedding" were thrown at a photographer responding to word association, the image evoked would be that of an imposing 4x5 Graphic bristling with accessories. If the image were to include for example, the unimpressively sized Rollei the consternation produced would be great! Alas! I am among the tainted—a user of small cameras, so read on at the risk of contamination!

2¼x2¼, 1⅝x2¼, 2¼x 3¼, 2¼x2¾, Sizes

Shooting candid weddings with a 4x5 camera can be compared to using a five-ton truck for a two-ton load. One practical solution to the problems created by the bulky 4x5 lies in the roll film camera.

If you are careful with your composition and are shooting only for yourself, the smaller camera offers a wide choice to select from. It is necessary that I stress, "shooting for yourself." Studios that hire photographers to shoot candid weddings are willing to pay the difference in cost between roll and sheet film. It is a small price to pay for the security that a 4x5 negative provides—especially when the not too experienced "professional" exposes a "2x3" portion of his 4x5 film.

Even if a studio were to consider the advantages (in dollars) of the roll film camera it would be confronted with an impasse: almost without exception all free lance photographers have the 4x5 that studios insist they own. With studios, the 4x5 is here to stay—at least for the present.

So if you are thinking of adding to your income by shooting candids both for studios and for yourself, buy a 4x5 and a good roll film camera. The 4x5 can be used for studio assignments; the roll film for your own weddings. Having two cameras should offer no hardship. No candid man should undertake to shoot a wedding without a substitute camera. In candid wedding work you've had it the first time—there are no retakes!

If the roll film camera is going to make an inroad into the candid wedding field, the example will have to be set by the candid men or less busy neighborhood studio owners shooting jobs of their own. They are not restricted to the 4x5. But most photographers are creatures of convention who go strictly by the book. They reason that the large studios must know best and have not thought to explore for themselves the possibilities of the roll film camera. They mistrust the ability of anything so small as a roll film negative. They are so wrong! Paradoxically, many of these same photographers will swear by the 2¼x2¼ reflex as the perfect camera for baby sittings.

Why Roll Film Cameras Are Suitable

As far as candids are concerned, the expensive, precision roll film camera, reflex or rangefinder, can produce photos equal in quality and sharpness to those taken with a 4x5. And only normal treatment is required to make fine-grain 8x10 or 11x14 enlargements from roll film negatives.

The finest camera artists in the fashion and editorial fields have driven home this point by their consistent use of the roll film camera to produce much of the high standard photography we see in our top publications. Even the newspapers are discovering the roll film camera and are getting to depend upon it more and more. A short time ago they would have considered anything less than 4x5 as amateur equipment.

Automatic film advance with simultaneous shutter cocking, double-exposure prevention, and lack of weight and bulk make the smaller camera an ideal instrument for candid weddings. As for graininess, there is no preceptible difference between a print made from 4x5 Tri-X film pack or Royal Pan sheet film developed in DK-50 and that made from a Tri-X, 2¼x2¼ negative developed in Microdol. The difference of cost between 4x5 and roll film is a revelation. A wedding can be shot on roll film (60 exposures) for about $2. With sheet film the cost would be about $6; film pack, $12.50! Film processing with roll film is simple and manufacturers offer developing tanks to fill every need. The Nikor tank in particular comes in several sizes to accommodate from one to eight reels of 120 or 620.

All right, you are convinced that the roll film camera is for you. But what about the public? Will the bridal couple lose confidence in a photographer with just a handful of camera? Let's ask the man who owns one.

About two years ago it occurred to me that no one had ever commented on the size of my stereo camera so on my next black-and-white job I shot one roll with my 2V4x2Y4 reflex during the wedding reception. I had no doubts concerning the quality of those negatives, but how would the couple react to my reflex? To my surprise, they didn't! I used the reflex more and more—still no reaction. About a year ago, I began using the reflex for the entire candid wedding. Every now and then an amateur will express mild surprise that my camera is not a Speed Graphic, or another candid man will assume that I am an amateur pursuing my hobby and patronizingly assure me that, "There's nothing like a Graphic."

A between-the-lens, fully synchronized MX shutter is more suited to flash photography than the focal-plane shutter, which is usually limited to a 1/25 to 1/50 second shutter speed with electronic flash or the M-type bulb. And a coupled rangefinder or reflex focusing are imperative for sharp pictures of bride, bride and groom, and group "formals."

An f/3.5, the most popular lens in 120 or 620 roll film cameras, is fast enough to cover any shot that is expected. A good lens with four or more elements will usually produce clearly defined eyes on all subjects in a group.

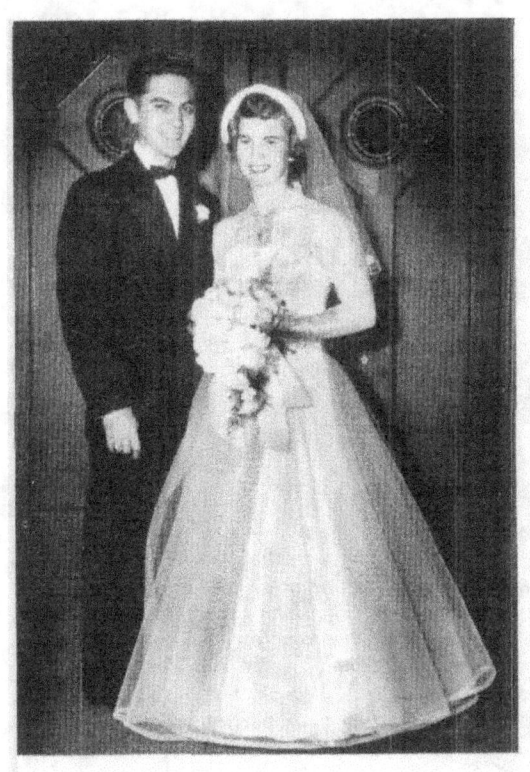

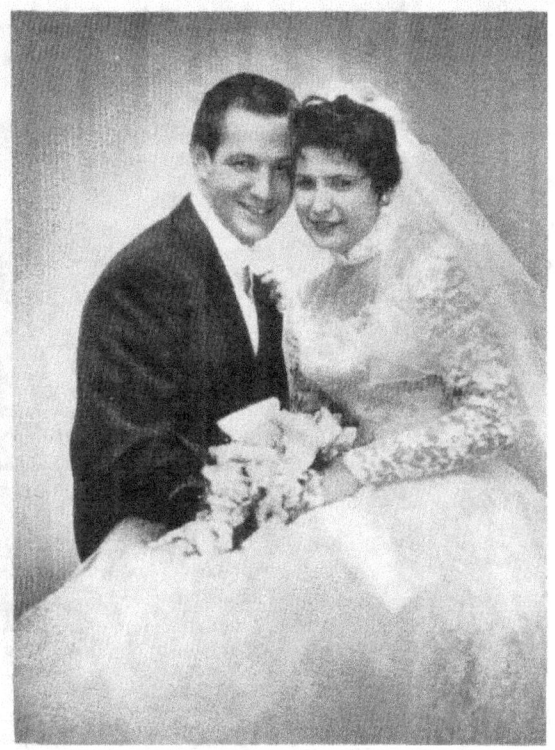

45. *The most popular pose of the bride and groom together is this full-length (left). Be sure that the groom is not so close to the bride that he interferes with the natural draping of the gown. Have him place his hand on the .small of the bride's hack and not completely around her waist. Check that the bride is holding her bouquet, that her gown is attractively draped, that the groom's tie is straight and his suit collar is correctly hanging. (Busch Pressman; Tri-X; 80 w/s electronic flash, 1/200 second, f/13; DK-50.)* 46. *The three-quarter length portrait (right) may be less formal. It may he taken with the couple either sitting or standing or even with the bride sitting and the groom standing. The couple may look at the camera as in this photograph, they may look at each other, at the bride's flowers or at her wedding ring. (Rolleiflex; Tri-X; 80 w/s electronic flash unit, partial bounce, 1/250 second, f/8; film developed in Microdol.)*

47. *My usual arrangement of the whole wedding party is illustrated in the photo across the page. When there are more than six in the wedding party I pose the bride and groom and then the maid of honor and best man. Then I stand the ushers on either side arranged by height, then I seat the bridesmaids in front of their respective ushers. The ring bearer or flower girl may be placed on either end of the group. If the feet of the seated girls show have them cross their ankles. For outdoor groups such as this I keep six camp stools in my car. With good grouping you achieve a compact composition; figures are larger and faces are clearer. (Busch Pressman; Tri-X; synchro-sunlight, 80 w/s electronic flash unit, 1/200, f/16; DK-50.)*

The Two Types of Roll Film Cameras

Roll film cameras can be classified in two groups: the non-reflex and reflex. The non-reflex is usually made with a collapsible bellows and a rigid metal lens mount. This collapsible camera can be folded for ease in carrying. In the expensive makes all have coupled rangefinders and fully synchronized MX shutters.

The reflex field is divided into single- and twin-lens reflex cameras. Because of the focal-plane shutter usually found on the single-lens reflex, the decision should go to the twin-lens model with its fully synchronized MX shutter.

As to preference between the reflex or rangefinder camera, ordinarily, the rangefinder would have the edge for faster and more accurate focusing. But public demand for the reflex has resulted in a more generous selection of precision twin-lens than rangefinder roll film cameras. One specific combination, the superbly machined Rolleiflex with its sportsfinder and accessory coupled rangefinder (Rolleimeter) is the equal of any rangefinder camera. The Kalart Focuspot (works same as Focuspot on press cameras) is another focusing aid for many reflexes. Two beams of light are projected on the subject. When they are superimposed, you are in focus. In norm ally-lighted rooms the Focuspot is useful up to about fifteen feet, in dimly-lit rooms, twenty-five feet is not too far.

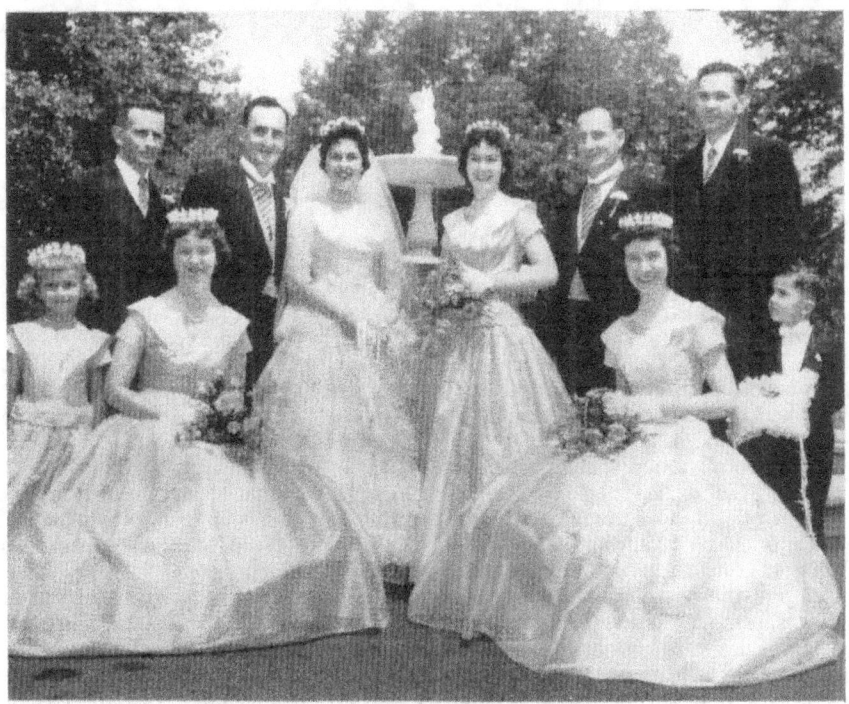

Even without these focusing accessories, the preference of rangefinder over reflex, where candids are concerned, is a matter of individual choice. There is no lack of light either in the home or reception room or at the well-lighted altar. Necklaces, earrings, and reflecting sequins are excellent for reflex focusing and in candlelight ceremonies, use the candles themselves.

2¼x2¼ (12 shots on 120 or 620 film)

Other than the 35mm the 2¼x2¼ is the most popular camera sold. Competition in this field has produced many fine cameras, but mostly of the reflex-type. Choice in the more expensive rangefinder type is very limited. Well-known examples are: the twin-lens Rolleiflex and the rangefinder Ikonta 4. The 2¼x2¼ is especially suited for shooting weddings. Twelve shots on a roll will require only two, or at most three, film changes when working with two cameras. The square format eliminates the necessity for shooting a horizontal or vertical composition. That choice is made on the enlarging easel.

1⅝x2¼ (16 exposures on 120)

The 1⅝x2¼ camera can be placed in the same class as the 2¼x2¼. However, with this size, composition must be determined at the time the shot is taken. The film size is slightly narrower than the portion of a 2¼x2¼ used to make an 8x10 enlargement. This camera takes sixteen exposures on a 120 roll and is worth considering especially for shooting the ceremony. The 16 exposures will eliminate the necessity of a second camera in church. With this size camera, choice is limited.

2¼x3¼ (8 exposures on 120 or 620 film)

This size film can be used for candids but has several drawbacks. First, more frequent film changes are required than with 2¼x2¼. Second, almost all candid wedding photos are enlarged to 8x10. So for convenience the view-finder should be masked to give a 2¼x2¾ negative that will conform with this paper size. However, the longer than necessary 100mm to 105mm lens for a film size masked down to 2¼x2¾ can make it difficult to shoot full-length photos in smaller living rooms.

Several cameras in this film size are constructed to give in addition to 2¼x3¼, 12 2¼x2¼ or 16 1⅝x2¼ exposures. This further reduction of film size increases still more the telephoto effect of the lens and is undesirable for house, reception and group shots. If you have a choice, avoid the 2¼x2¼ roll film camera. The disadvantages are many; the advantages none.

For the photographer who has jobs during the week which require only a few shots, an excellent compromise is the relatively light 2¼x3¼, miniature press. Film pack (about the same cost as 4x5 sheet film), sheet film and economical roll film can be used. It is particularly suited for roll films as holders are available that can be loaded in advance and slipped on and off as simply and rapidly as a film pack adapter. These holders are obtainable for 2¼x3¼, (8 exposures) or 2¼x2¼ (12 exposures). As was the case with the 2¼x3¼, the viewfinder will have to be masked down to the 2¼x2¾ or 2¼x2¼ format. A mask is available for the telescopic finder. The coupled rangefinder is a necessary accessory for this camera. The miniature press, when fully equipped, comes with a 100 to 105mm lens that can be used but is a longer focal-length than needed for the usable 2¼x2¾ portion of the film and much too long for the 2¼x2¼ size. The miniature press has a removable lens board, making a choice of lenses possible. A 90mm lens is "normal" for 2¼x2¾. Wollensak makes this focal length in f/4.5. The 80mm **f/8.3** Kodak Wide Field Ektar (discontinued, but still to be found) would be a good choice. It gives the smaller 2¼x2¼ picture a normal field of view, and the 2¼x2¾ a moderate wide-angle effect, but corner to corner coverage. Using this lens the 2¼x3¾ roll film holder (with viewfinder masked to 2¼x2¾) could be your choice in the house, and for bridal groups; with 2¼x2¾ masking, for church and reception. The f/6.3 lens, with a smaller (60-watt-second) electronic flash unit, will not "make it" to the altar of larger churches, and with shots like "throwing the bouquet." An 80-watt-second input unit is needed for an efficient job. Psychologically (for the photographer who thinks it necessary) the small press camera is effective in that it resembles the professional looking 4x5.

Other Sizes

Before the introduction of fine-grain film and developers, and precision enlargers, most picture taking was done on large film and ended in a contact print. Now, the serious photographer, amateur as well as professional, exposes a negative for future enlargement to 8x10 or more. This condition has caused two camera manufacturers to re-evaluate the practicality of the odd-size 2¼x3¼ negative and introduce in its place the realistic $2^{1/4}x2^{3/4}$ proportions that make an 8x10 enlargement without waste of film. The Omega 120 (9 exposures on 120 film) with 90mm lens is one (if only it had a removable back like the Hasselblad's); the other is the Graflex 70mm Combat Camera with its 50-exposure cassette, spring motor drive, automatic film advance and shutter-cocking, built-in film sheer, etc. It is the answer to a wedding photographer's dream with one substitution: the use of between-the-lens shutter in place of the present focal-plane so that electronic flash or Class M bulbs might be used at all speeds for synchro-sunlight photos. This camera was originally designed and manufactured for the Signal Corps. The focal-plane shutter is needed for the three interchangeable, barrel-mount lenses. There is a limited surplus available for the public. So you rush to your dealer, see it—want it, focal-plane shutter or no! (You can always use that second camera for the few synchro-sunlight photos.) But remember this dream camera, with a 4-inch f/2.8 Ektar, "is such stuff as dreams are made on." Eighteen hundred and fifty dollars worth!

At any rate, the number of features the Graflex 70mm has incorporated, features found only in the 35mm class, portend wondrous advances to be expected in the press camera of the future. How far in the future depends on the advanced amateur. Professionals exert an important influence on what the amateur will choose but they constitute an unimportant percentage of the total camera buyers. It is faith in the amateur's readiness to accept a new or improved piece of equipment, and faith in his ample purse that induces a manufacturer to undertake the cost of designing, tooling and producing a new model. For proof that the amateur is "king" to the manufacturer, consider the 35mm camera. An enormous number of higher-priced 35's are sold today. This market is so lucrative and competition so keen, that no matter what combination of features you desire, it's an even bet your dealer carries the camera that has them. So, the next time you see an amateur with a Leica M-3 or Rol-lei 2.8E shooting into the sun without a lens-shade, suppress that guffaw, approach him with deference. Take off your hat and cast a protective shadow over his lens. Due him, is the credit for that intricate instrument hanging from your own shoulder.

A Matter of Choice

Off that cloud and down to earth! What is the best roll film camera for candid weddings? Any one of a dozen good cameras with fully synchronized MX shutter will do, but I'm afraid you will find most of them in the reflex field. In the rangefinder group the pickings are poor: the Ikontas focus by varying the distance between the lens elements—a feature not conducive to the sharpest pictures. The Mamiya folding camera has a satisfactory body and its Olympus lens is excellent. It can be adjusted to take, in addition to the 2¼ square, 16 1⅝x2¼ negatives on the 120 roll. The discontinued automatic Kodak Chevron, though bulky, came closest to what might be expected of a really good roll film rangefinder camera.

The press-type Omega 120? You couldn't do better were it not for the nuisance of changing film every 9 exposures. As a matter of fact, a camera like

48. *A group such as this may have an informal air even though it is obviously posed. It may be set up either indoors or out, with the parents of the couple on either side, or with the women seated and the men standing. The subjects may be looking at the camera or at each other. When as large an area is included as in the picture opposite, watch to be certain that no one walks into the background of the picture. (Rolleiftex; Tri-X; synchro-shade, 60 w/s electronic flash unit, 1/100 second, f/5.6; film developed in Microdol.)*

the Omega 120 with a back like the Hasselblad would probably make an ideal candid wedding camera.

My *Personal Choice*

At present I use two types. One is the folding, bellows-type Maraiya 6 from Japan. I like this camera particularly for the church shots because of its 16 1⅝x2¼ frames on a roll of 120 film. On an average I only need 14 shots in the church and 16 gives me a margin of 2 pictures. Furthermore the negative size is just about right for tin 8x10 enlargement because the proportions are nearly the same. The camera has a good, sharp Olympus f/3.5 lens, and eyes on my subjects show up clearly in shots made at 12 to 15 feet and enlarged to 8x10. I also use the twin-lens Rolleinex continually. Of course there are many other good twin-lens cameras to choose from: the Rolleicord, Ikofiex (with Tessar lens), Kalloflex, Minolta Autocord, Mamiyaflex, Aires Automat, and Tele-Koniflex. Any of these will take top quality pictures. Too, the twin-lens reflex is a solid camera, capable of taking the strenuous treatment of a candid wedding. Focusing is a little more difficult than with a rangefinder camera, but not enough to make a serious difference. And with a twin-lens reflex you

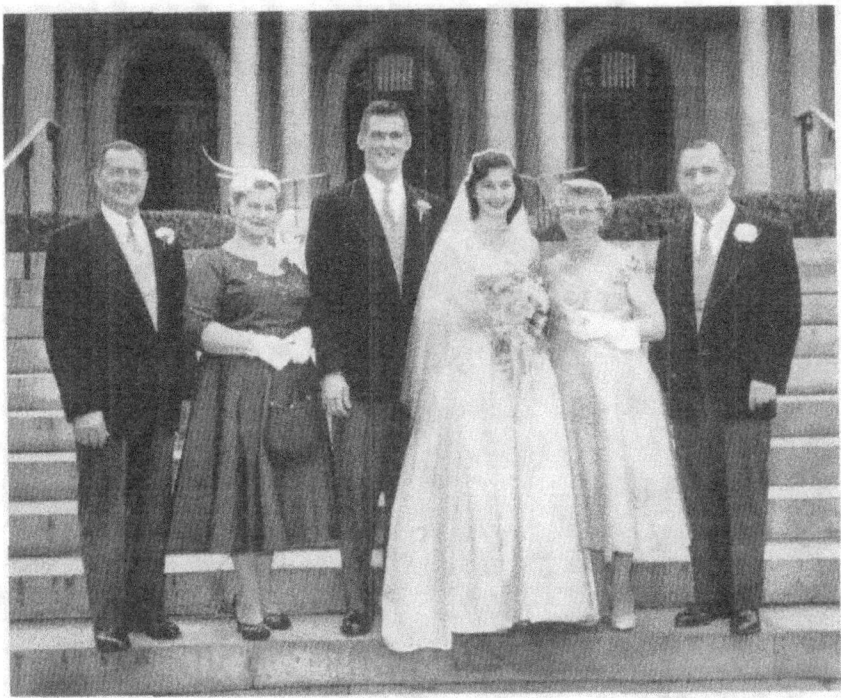

have an added bonus—you are equipped to photograph the bride and groom now, and their baby later.

So I'll take the Rolleiflex. It is the camera I most like to live with today. Equipped with an f/3.5 or f/2.8 lens and the accessory rangefinder (Rollei-meter) it is the camera without a fault.

Without a fault? Well . . . the Rolleimeter (rangefinder) is a useful accessory, but I've often wondered if designers of equipment ever use their own brainchildren. Attached to the Rollei the activating arm of the Rolleimeter is directly above the indicator window however, in poor light conditions, at a time when the rangefinder is needed most the diaphragm numbers can not be read. Burleigh Brooks was kind enough to grind away a portion of the arm directly over the window, but that helped little. I took the Rollei to a camera repair shop and had them drill a burr on the face of the lens mount on the side closest to the diaphragm wheel. On the wheel itself six burrs were drilled, one for each f/stop. The indentations were painted black. Now I just refer to the dots on the diaphragm wheel and not to the window. This operation was not repeated on the shutter speed wheel. The click stops let you know what speed you are using. With this slight modification; I guess I still say, "The camera without a fault."

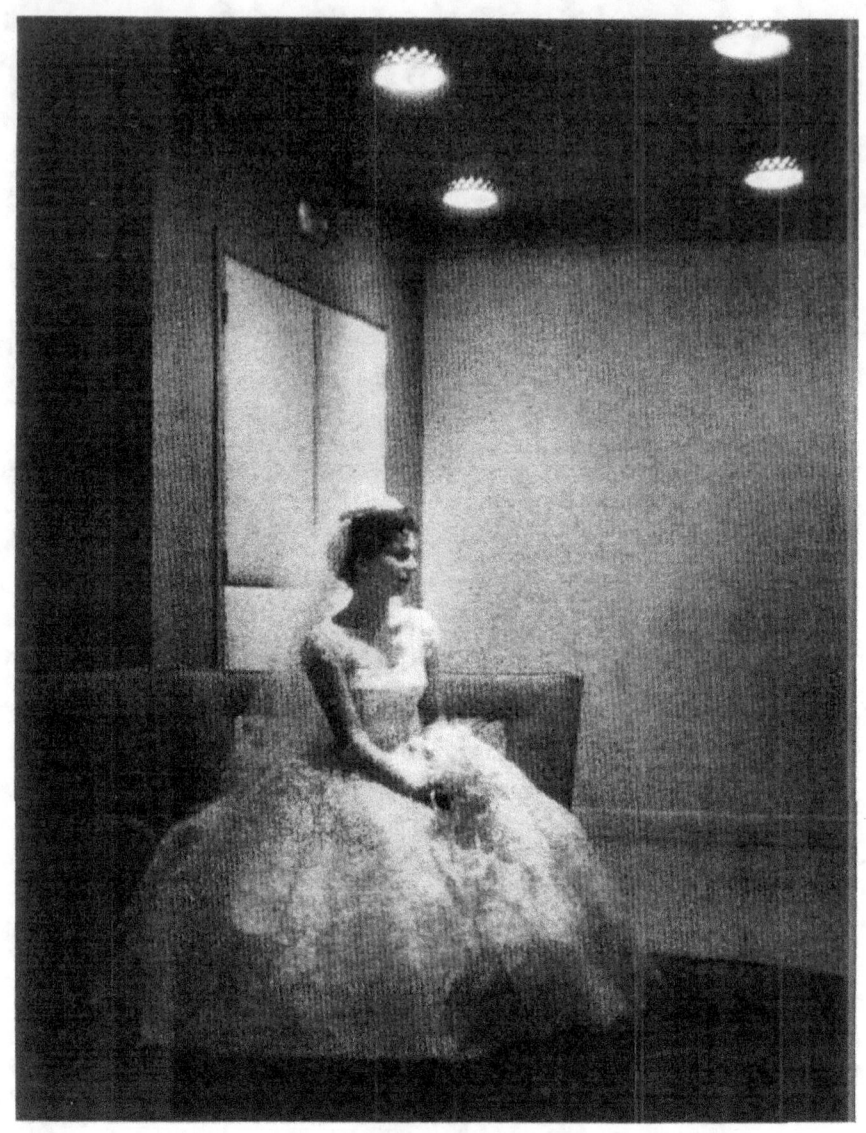

49. *Couples are frequently receptive if a few pictures with imagination are included in the wedding coverage. The formal portrait above was made while the bride was waiting for the ceremony (Jewish) to begin. Tri-X film was purposely over-exposed by two stops (1/30, f/1.8) and force developed. The dense, grainly negative and the wide open aperture produced the soft, textured, dreamy effect. (Nikon; 35mm Nikkor.)*

8.

35 mm Cameras

So 35MM CAMERA is all you have and you want to know where you stand in this business of candid wedding photography. If your camera lens will reproduce eyes clearly in a twelve foot flash shot, you are equipped to shoot. By today's high standards this is but a minimum requirement for the medium-priced camera. Top-priced cameras no longer hold a monopoly on fine picture making. Negatives from a Leica M-3 or the very much less expensive Konica III, or the Retina IIC are equal as far as the candid wedding photographer is concerned.

How do prices range for good 35mm cameras? All the way from about $50 up into the $400-$500 bracket. In between, however, are many fine cameras at medium prices. Today you can get a precision 35mm camera with five-element, f/2.8 lens for about $70-$100; or a camera with a six-element f/1.9 or f/2 lens for between $100 and $120. Many of the best buys are made in Japan.

About Lenses

Paradoxically, it was misuse of the older f/2 (and faster) lenses that did much to compromise the reputation of the 35mm camera. Even now, the higher price of a faster lens does not predicate sharper pictures. Fast or super-fast lenses are intended for just one purpose—as an indispensable tool for the man who must shoot under low-light level conditions. Used wide open an f/1.4 lens does not provide the resolution of a good f/3.5 wide open. (Elgeet's introduction of a mass-produced aspheric movie lens gives promise of greater resolution at open apertures for high-speed lenses of the future.)

The average amateur has the mistaken notion that the faster and consequently more expensive the lens, the sharper the picture. It takes him time to concede that this impressive hunk of glass for which he paid an arm and a leg, is less critical at maximum aperture than his old f/3.5 or f/4.5; and that come to think of it, he has very little use for larger lens openings than f/5.6. At the other end of the scale are the inexpensive cameras with their ineffectual two- and mediocre three-element lenses. They, too, have done much to belittle the reputation of the "35."

75

Picture Quality and the "35"

Now for the final degradation. . . . The 35mm, unlike its bigger brother the roll film negative, is small and of a sensitive character. Farmed off to the uncaring hands of the local drug store, forsaken by its parent, fed a diet of harsh solutions—is it any wonder that the 35mm frame develops into a grainy and gray picture?

Is it all hopeless? Not by a long shot. There is one shining light—the advanced amateur (and, of course, that glamorous creature, the professional who works with a "35"). Experience has taught him that the slower f/8.5 or f/2.8 is fast enough for flash or daylight exposures. His solutions are fresh and his exposures close. He is the exception who proves by pictures and not talk that a sharp 8x10 or 11x14, without objectionable grainmess, can be made with material stocked by the neighborhood stationery or drug store—Plus-X and Microdol. With Panatomic-X, brother, give him room—he's out for the large and not the economy sizes.

To prove this point of quality, along with a bunch of 8x10 candid pictures made from 4x5 or roll film negatives, include several made from 35mm Plus-X developed in Microdol. The average person will look at them as pictures, noting no difference. The professional would be splitting hairs in pointing out the slight graininess.

Pros *and Cons*

Then why not use a "35" for black and white candids? I don't have to! I have other cameras that will do the job better. Remember, this is my livelihood, so why should I do it the hard way? You are the boy with one camera. I say you are equipped, or better still can get along with the "35". Certainly the elongated 35mm frame is not a comfortable shape for making 8x10's. Packaged 20 exposure film is no cheaper per shot than film for 2¼x2¼ exposures and little cheaper in the 36. For me, there is a slight difference in weight, but no mechanical advantage in a "35" over the reflexes I use. Tele-photo and extreme wide angle lenses are not essential for shooting a candid wedding. The one most enviable advantage with the "35" is fewer film changes with the 20 or 36 exposure magazine.

In terms of a hobby you are set. For weddings, I do not recommend the "35", other than as a useful piece of supplementary equipment. With an f/2 or faster lens, high speed film and powerful medium fine-grain developers, exposures of 1/25 (or even action-stopping 1/50 or 1/60) will be possible where use of flash is prohibited as is the case with many churches.

Today's films and developers, plus cameras of watchlike precision have made the taking of excellent photographs with 35mm film a simple matter. The "35's" greatest testimonial is its universal acceptance in professional fields. It is the camera of pictorial weeklies, an important tool of fashion illustrators. It is responsible for many of the pictures in your Sunday paper.

For ease of operation this midget has no peer. Its one limitation is film size, and if we admit this limitation and take care in filling our negative and in exposure and development, this obstacle can be satisfactorily surmounted.

Directly applied to candids the more expensive 35mm cameras offer the following mechanical advantages:

1. Ease of handling; principally size of the box.

2. Fast lenses: f/1.1 to f/3.5. If you do not shoot under low light-level conditions buy an f/2.8 or f/3.5 lens and save a lot of money.

3. A choice of rangefinder, waist-level reflex, eye-level prism reflex focus ing, or the ideal combination of rangefinder and reflex on one camera. In not too bright areas, the rangefinder is faster and more accurate to use.

4. Tremendous depth of field.

5. Choice of 20 or 36 shots in one loading—great for candids as it mini mizes the nuisance of reloading.

6. Interchangeably of lenses: wide angle and telephoto, provide an almost limitless versatility.
a—Use the wide angle (35mm) for the close areas of smaller rooms.
b—Use the telephoto (85 or 135mm) for % length portraits.

However, accessory lenses are not indispensable; the photographer shooting a candid wedding and using flash can get along with a "normal 45mm to 58mm focal length and a maximum aperture of f/3.5. But, if I were given a choice of just one lens, I would select the less restricting 35mm focal-length as the most comfortable lens for shooting candids. Admittedly, there is some danger of distortion with a shorter-than-"normal" focal-length but it is nothing that a little care won't circumvent. With wide-angle lenses, make certain your flash reflector will cover a 65-degree angle of view. The 35mm lens with a 35mm camera is no less "normal" than the popular combination of 127mm lens (made to cover 3¼x4¼) and 4x5 camera.

The "35V *Shutter*

The focal-plane shutter is common with cameras that provide for inter-changeable lenses as in the Leica, Contax, Nikon and others. Top speeds of 1/500 or 1/1000 are usual. Because of its construction and operation, the focal-plane shutter cannot be used with electronic flash at speeds higher than 1/25 or 1/50 second. And the focal-plane shutter is usually not compatible with Class M No. 5 or 25 bulbs at speeds above 1/25 and 1/50. An FP (focal plane) flashbulb must be used at fast shutter speeds. Indoors with electronic flash, the slow shutter speeds pose no important problem to the wedding photographer. The brief duration of the speedlight (1/500 to 1/2000) and not the shutter determines the exposure. The effect is action-stopping open flash.

Between-the-lens MX shutters are used on cameras with fixed lenses. The Konica III and the Retina IIC are of this class. The X setting is for speedlight; the M for Class M flashbulbs. The No. 5 or No. 25 are two such bulbs. All the new, expensive cameras with between-the-lens MX shutters are fully synchro-nized—meaning, flashbulbs or electronic flash can be used at all shutter speeds.

A third type of shutter, though not yet so popular as the previous two, is the behind-the-lens type. It is a compromise between the focal plane and the between-the-lens shutter. It is intended to afford the focal plane's advantage of interchangeability of lenses and the MX's full synchronization. It is just what the name implies, "behind-the-lens." The Diax IIb is an example in the more expensive class and the Argus C-44 in the middle price field.

General Suggestions

The 35mm viewfinder should be masked or allowance made to give a Ixiy4-inch instead of lxl½-inch frame. This is to provide for 8x10 enlargements (the standard size for the slip-in type candid wedding album) without having to cut off the feet of your subjects or the people at the end of the group.

If you use a dry-mount type of wedding book either the full frame can be used and all photos trimmed to correspond with the 35mm proportions; or each photograph may be cut to dimensions you feel best contain the subject matter.

For daylight or flash, Plus-X developed in Microdol is an excellent compromise insofar as film speed, exposure latitude, shadow detail, fine grain and high acutance (sharpness) are concerned. (D-76 will produce generally the same results, but with a slight increase in graininess.) Tri-X will give acceptable results when most of the negative is utilized and 8x10 is the maximum enlargement, but is likely to appear grainy if there is considerable cropping of the negative or 11x14 enlargements are made. Super fine-grain Panatomic-X will give superlative results, but flashbulbs will have to be used if your electronic flash is less than a 100-watt-second unit. Also to be kept in mind: the slower films often produce greater contrast and are usually more constricted in exposure latitude. When you enlarge 35mm film, a double or even triple condenser enlarger and a fine enlarging lens are a necessity. I would avoid the diffusion or cold light systems.

9

Film and Film Development

FOR HIGH-PRICED CAMERAS, roll and 35mm, we depend largely on either Japan or Germany. This is inconsistent in a country that produces the finest film and uses the most of it. But the film facts remain: just name your film needs and we've got it, both in variety and quality, labeled U.S.A. (With this I'll take a precautionary step backward to avoid the brickbats from Adox and Ilford converts.)

All major film manufacturers offer some films that can be used for candid weddings. Ansco has Supreme and Superpan Press. Kodak has all that we can use and in all film sizes from very high speed Royal-X Pan for sheet film, to Tri-X or Royal Pan (exposure index 200-160) through medium-speed (exposure index 80-64) excellent contrast Verichrome Pan or Plus-X down to Panatomie-X (exposure index 25-20) whose ultrafine-grain, high resolution and thin emulsion are capable of producing superlative image quality.

Whatever the make of film you choose, if it's a name brand (domestic or foreign) the manufacturer will not let you down. But, if photography is your livelihood or an important money maker, the purchase of each material cannot become a project. The hackneyed expression, "Time is money," holds true. Film (and other supplies) for our "bread and butter" work should be simple to buy. And in this country, that usually means either from Eastman or Ansco. My personal choice in film for a long time has been:

4x5: Tri-X Film Pack, or Royal Pan Sheet Film with a 60- to 80-watt second electronic flash. (You will need this film speed for partial-bounce and electronic flash. At 12 feet your lens opening will be f/4.5, with a 60-watt-second unit, and f/7 with an 80-watt-second unit. Kodak's Super Panchro-Press, Type B, or Verichrome Pan (film pack only) with No. 5 bulb or 100-watt-second (or stronger) electronic flash.

120 or 620: Tri-X with a 60- to 80-watt-second electronic flash unit. Verichrome Pan with a 100-watt-second unit or a No. 5 bulb.

35-tnm Plus-X for all flash. Tri-X with available light (forced development). Quality-wise and contrast-wise I prefer it to the faster British Ilford HPS. You may have a different preference and you should experiment, of course, with faster films as they are released. Panatomic-X is a sensitive prima donna. Its fine image quality depends on accurate exposures (within safety factor). Extended development produces excessive contrast. Other than for formals (indoor or outdoor) or in other situations where care can be taken, I would forget Panatomic-X or any of the thin-emulsion ultra-fine grain films. However if Panatomic-X is used, D-76 will give good results. Microdol has a tendency to dissolve the periphery of each grain, giving fine grain, but an illusion of slightly less sharpness than is expected from this film. With other fine-grain, thin-emulsion films, I have found that a compensating developer like FR's X-22 really does preserve fine grain, high resolution and good gradation.

Other Comments

Royal Pan film has the same speed and characteristics as Tri-X film pack, though not the same developing times. Plus-X and Verichrome Pan have the same tonal characteristics as the faster Tri-X though more contrast, and provide better shadow detail. In the Kodak products, do not confuse the Type B, Tri-X film pack with the older, Type C, Tri-X sheet film. They are not the same.

Repeated use of the same materials and equipment is a good practice. Shooting a candid need not be nerve wracking it you know exactly what your film, flash and camera can do. A photographer can not do justice to posing, facial expressions or to exposing the truly candid shots at the right moment if the mechanical aspects of taking a picture are not automatic.

Film Development

Unfortunately, there is no one ideal contrast for candid wedding negatives. Contrast must be adjusted to suit subject matter, lighting, locale and your particular enlarging system. (See Chapter 10 on Enlargers and Printing.) Candids present us with a difficult challenge. Included in almost every photo are two extremes: the white of the bridal gown and the black of hair or male attire, with the off-whites of flesh tones somewhere in-between.

Ordinarily a negative on the soft side would be the answer but straight flash is flat and some overdevelopment is needed with full-length figures to avoid muddy flesh tones. As a rule, this favoring of flesh tones will produce whites that are slightly chalky. One practical way to control this incompatibility is with a variable contrast paper of which DuPont's Varigam is the pioneer. Softness and detail can be introduced by burning-in the whites through a No. 3 filter (equal to a No. 1 paper contrast).

Unlike straight flash, partial bounce (see illustration 5) poses no processing problem. Softness, modeling and shadow detail are characteristic of this light. Developing film 30 percent more than for straight flash causes flesh tones, the whites and the blacks all to fall into a harmonious relationship. Straight printing and burning-in on a No. 2 paper, or with Varigam and no filter, will produce an excellent print.

Locale also plays an important part in deciding the length of film development. Flash, in large areas such LS churches and halls (generally all shots over 15 feet) requires 30 percent more development than straight flash (up to 12 feet). This provides enough contrast for printing on a No. 2 paper.

The contention may be voiced that all film can be developed for one time, and contrast controlled by softer or harder papers. This method may leave us out on a limb in case of accidental over- or under-exposure, or over- or under-development. We are not as secure as the man whose exposures are intended for a No. 2 paper, and is thereby protected by the bracketing contrast grades of No. 0, 1, 3, and 4 papers, and. sometimes by No. 5.

Admittedly, it is difficult, even with sheet film, to develop every exposure of a candid so it will print on a No. 2 paper. With roll film it is often impractical if not impossible. But the closer we stay to the No. 2 grade the easier it will be to handle this most difficult expression of photography—the candid wedding story.

How to *Develop Film in Quantity*

When I used 4x5 film, I developed 50 to 120 negatives at one time using a gallon of fresh developer. In candids, negative development of sheet film with hangers is safe though time consuming. The tray method I employed is a rapid way of processing from one "to two entire candid weddings in less than one half an hour. For me, it has proved as safe as hanger developing. To get the "feel" I suggest buying some outdated sheet film and film packs and going through the complete process with the lights on.

This is how it's done. Use 3 oval trays or baby baths about 18x15x5 inches. Place them side by side. Starting from the left, fill the first with exactly one gallon of water. Add 1 capful of Kodak Wetting agent (it is the wetting agent that keeps the film from sticking). Behind this tray place a wide-mouthed bottle with a gallon of (undiluted) DK-50, and an 8x10 tray of water containing $V\backslash$ capful of wetting agent.

In the second oval tray prepare a gallon and a half of short stop. In the third oval tray place about a gallon and a half of hypo. The water with wetting agent and the developer must be at 68F. The short stop and hypo can vary within 4 degrees either way.

You will need two timers and a Kodak Safelight filter (Wratten Series 3, dark green). Though not essential, the safelight allows three or four brief inspections after development is half completed! and will be of help when time comes to transfer film from developer tray to short stop and later hypo. So if your film (say, Royal Pan) was exposed by electronic flash set one timer for two minutes and one for nine and a half.

Now put out the lights and place your two boxes of film—one with all the straight flash shots (made under 12 feet) and all synchro-sunlight pictures; the other with those of the church, reception, mirror shots, large group pictures and partial bounce—to the left of the first tray. Keep the film face down (easier to pick up and to avoid fingerprints).

Now one by one put all the straight-flash house and small group shots (made under 12 feet) into the water of the 8x10 tray. Rock for one minute. In the same manner put the rest of film from the other box into the large oval tray with water. Rock for one minute and a half then push the film to one end of the tray. Start both clocks. Pour the gallon of stock developer into the end of the oval tray away from the film, and rock actively, frequently changing directions until the first timer rings. Then, all at once, pick up the film from the 8x10 tray and drop it into the developer. Continue active rocking for one more minute then settle down to a moderate pace. During the entire developing your other hand keeps feeling for film that might climb up the sides of the tray (this seldom occurs with sheet film) and also gently pushes all the film circle-wise. Now and then move one finger along the bottom of the tray and let the film tap against it. When the second bell rings, push your developer tray against the short stop tray. Turn on your safelight. Pick up the firm, all at once if possible, and dump it into the short stop. Then turn off the safe-light. Use the same agitation method as in developing, for two minutes, then finally put the film into the hypo and agitate for four minutes.

Turn on the light. (Don't look at the film, but at your hair—it might be white!) Relax! If you've kept your fingernails to yourself you'll have a batch of beautiful negatives. Agitate in hypo five more minutes. Wash for ten minutes, using a Kodak Syphon or similar tray-type washer. Proceed to hang the film, but meanwhile, keep the wash water running. If the wash water is hard add an eyedropper full of wetting agent every two minutes. Do not sponge or wipe the film. From start to wash water this method takes less than 30 minutes.

A word of caution; Limit yourself to fifty films for the first ten times you develop, then, if you wish, add three or four films each time until you reach seventy-five (or even one hundred) and call it quits. (Later, for fifty films, you will find yourself working with half a gallon of water and half a gallon of developer.) How far can you go? I don't know, I normally developed about 120 sheet film and film pack exposures mixed—two candid weddings. However, I've been doing tray development for ten years; I don't own a hanger.

Developing Times with DK-50 (1:1)

(Continuous Agitation—Tray) 68 Degrees F

Film	Light	Time Straight flash: House & formals (made under 12 feet); also synchro-sunlight	Time Church, reception mirror & partial-bounce (shots over 12 feet)
Royal Pan	Electronic Flash	7½ min.	9½ min.
Tri-X film pack	"	7½ min.	9½ min.
Royal Pan	No. 5 flashbulb	7 min.	9 min.
Tri-X film pack		7 min.	9 min.

The reader may wonder at the identical developing times for Tri-X film pack and Royal Pan sheet film when normally Tri-X requires 2 minutes more with tray development and undiluted developer. Film pack emulsions have a protective coating to prevent abrasion as the film is drawn through the magazine. This coating resists the developer. Prewetting dissolves the coating and developing action takes place about as fast as with sheet film.

Developing by Inspection

Developing by inspection is a phase of photography that is indispensable to the available light photographer. Even in the course of everyday shooting a situation sometimes arises that leaves us in doubt as to the accuracy of our exposure. It is a comfort to know that you can look at the film during development and see "what's cooking." The simple solution, and in liquid form, is provided by the tongue twister pinakryptol green, or by the more easily pronounced Kodak Desensitizer. Essentially both serve the same purpose and instructions come with either product. There is nothing complicated to de-sensitization.

Prior to developing, soak your film in either of these desensitizers for a few minutes. The film can now be inspected during the course of development by regular paper safelight with pinakryptol green and by a Wratten Series 7 (light green) Safelight with the Kodak product. The pinakryptol green has a tendency to lengthen the developing time—with some developers as much as 50 percent. Kodak Desensitizer does not have this effect. For this reason I prefer the Kodak product.

Using it, practice desensitizing film which you know has been properly exposed and is to be developed by time and temperature. See what happens to this film during development and you will learn what to look for when the necessity arises for developing film by inspection alone. In time, when you have become proficient enough to limit yourself to three short 5-10 second inspections between halfway and full development points, change to a Wratten Series No. 3 and forget the desensitizer.

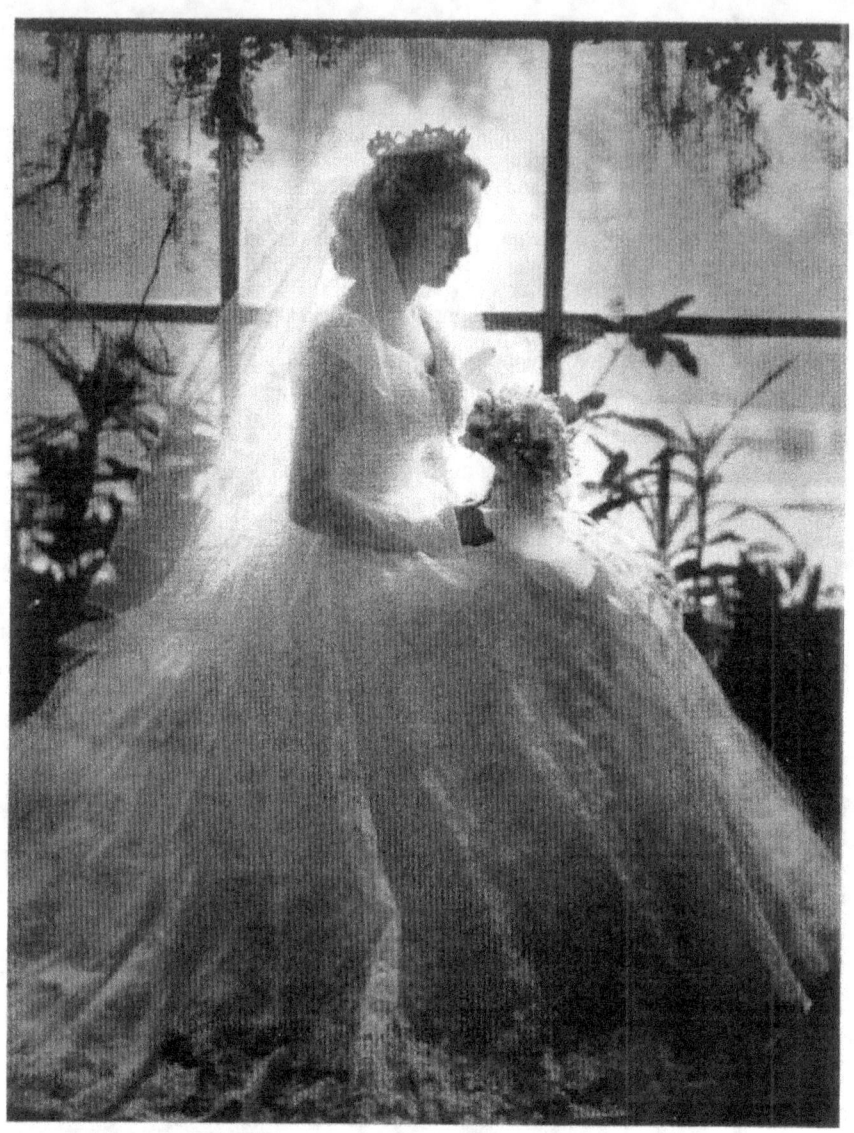

50. *The light from a cloudy day coming through the window in the hack-ground provided the illumination for this semi-silhouetted formal. (A completely different effect would have been obtained if supplementary flash had been used.) For this, a meter reading was taken from the shadow side of the gown. The 4x5 Royal-X Pan film was exposed at 1/25 and f/4.7. The film was tray developed for 9 minutes in DK-50. (Busch Pressman camera.)*

10

Enlargers and Printing Techniques

WITH ALL FILM from 4x5 to 35mm I prefer an enlarger with clear condensers and an opal enlarging lamp. With the developers prescribed and condenser enlargers there should be little or no graininess in reasonably sized enlargements made from roll or 4x5 film, and none that is objectionable with 35mm. I assume, too, that for the clean and careful worker the problem of dust and scratches can be minimized to nothing more than nuisance value. The condenser enlarger permits the use of a less dense negative than one required by a diffusion system. This, along with its inherent printing speed, is a great help with wedding photos where almost every picture requires considerable burning-in of bridal gown, bouquet or cake.

A second choice would be the cold light enlarger. The Aristo cold light heads are designed to fit most standard enlargers and provide a contrast about halfway between the diffusion and condenser systems. The HI (high-intensity) Aristo Grid Lamp is especially suited for the smaller enlargers. It produces a contrast and printing speed that is about equal to that of condensers. The HI Aristo deserves particular consideration. If you use a 4x5 negative and have a diffusion enlarger don't throw it away. With the proper contrast negative your work will not suffer. Your only penalty will be more time in the darkroom.

The Enlarging Lens

Coated camera lenses, as well as shutters internally synchronized for flash, were introduced about the time of World War II. Today there are few advanced photographers who use an uncoated lens. Greater contrast, improved tonal fidelity, resistance to flare are the important advantages of a coated taking lens.

The enlarging lens differs. Unless made obsolete by improved formulas, as was the case of the old rectilinear being replaced by the anastigmatic, the enlarging lens can be used indefinitely. The only effect coating has on an enlarging lens is a minor increase in picture contrast. In itself, the lack of coating is no reason for replacing an otherwise fine enlarging lens. The same care should be exercised in selecting an enlarging lens as for a camera lens.

The results of a sharp camera lens can be made mediocre by an inferior enlarging lens.

The Bask Enlarging Systems

The chart on the opposite page includes the basic enlarging systems, combinations of these systems, and their effect on film developing times.

Because of the color sensitivity of variable contrast papers, only enlarging systems should be used that employ regular opal enlarging lamps or certain "warm tone" fluorescent tubes. "Cold light" or daylight fluorescent tubes emit mainly blue light and upset the contrast range intended by the manufacturers for these papers, a range, that closely parallels the contrast grades of conventional papers. The developing times shown are based on negatives with a suitable contrast for printing on No. 2 paper. Varigam with a No. 5 filter, or no filter, is approximately equivalent to a No. 2 (normal) paper, or to Varigam High Speed.

To start, follow the figures in the chart for all No. 2 papers then gradually adjust your film development to suit your taste and to compensate for any variation in the paper you prefer.

The Incomparable Varigam

"Boil it, broil it, bleach it," was part of an incantation chanted repeatedly on radio and television. It warned against the abuse to which a woman's hair was subjected and implied that all need not be lost if the listener would only use her head and his product. I have forgotten the name of the product and the exact words of the spiel but "boil it, broil it, bleach it" has stuck and comes to mind often when I am working with DuPont's Varigam paper.

All of us are familiar, through ads and articles in photographic magazines, with the wonders that can be worked with this variable contrast paper—how it eliminates the need for three or four different grades of paper, how you use the same paper at all times, but change the filter through which the exposure is made to vary contrast. Filters range from 1 (soft) to 10 (hard). Amazing indeed! But no mention is made of its toughness, and resistance to treatment which would make most papers turn yellow and curl up their edges in dismay.

Most photographers do candids for money, some to help defray the expense of their hobby and a few strictly for pleasure. But all candid wedding men are confronted with the same problem: a very tough printing job. Almost every print deals with face and gown, then has to include the extreme other end of the scale—the black of hair and formal dress. To make a hard job harder, both the black clothes and white gown must have detail.

Little can be done to shorten the time it takes to shoot a candid wedding but something can be done to shorten the time of printing one. The ability to work rapidly in the darkroom means money to the professional, and to all photographers the satisfaction of being the masters of their material.

On the other hand, I have yet to see the man who could accurately expose a whole set of wedding prints, develop the prints all at once in regular or undiluted developer, and not have to remake at least half of them. But give a good printer a paper which can take torture, a tray of hot water, and one of ferricyanide solution, and he is only a step away from real printing

TYPE OF FLASH	ENLARGING SYSTEM	ENLARGING LAMP	COATED LENS	UNCOATED LENS	FILM DEVELOPING TIMES* Straight flash, house & formals (under 12 feet); Synchro-sunlight	FILM DEVELOPING TIMES* Church, reception, mirror shots, partial bounce, shots over 12 ft.
F	Condenser	Opal	X		5% less	
L	Condenser	"	X	X	Time recommended	
A	Diffusion	"			20% more	
S	Diffusion	"	X	X	30% more	THIRTY PERCENT MORE
H	Semi-diffusion: (with top condenser ground or with ground glass over condenser)	"	X		10% more	
B	Semi-diffusion (same as above)	"		X	20% more	
U	Cold Light (except HI Aristo)		X		20% more	
L	Cold Light (except HI Aristo)			X	30% more	
B	HI Aristo		X		5% less	
	HI Aristo			X	10% more	

* Longer or shorter developing times than those recommended by the manufacturer on the instruction sheet included with the film. Instructions regarding temperature, time, (above) and method of agitation should be rigidly followed. When electronic flash is used, add an extra 10 percent to developing times right down the line.

efficiency. Varigam is the paper you can torture, the paper that can "take it." It is custom-made for candid weddings. Prints that turn out poor or fair with conventional photographic papers can be improved with Varigam, the paper that can record on one sheet a range from No. 1 through No. 4 contrasts. To test Varigam]ets:

"Boil" It. (Hot Water)

For candid wedding photography where either white gown, bouquet or cake are in every picture hot water is an indispensable paper developing aid. Water at 120F can be used locally to bring up the detail in white areas that had insufficient burning-in. A two or three second dunking in water at 100F and back to developer can save a moderately underexposed print. Hot water will probably save 70 percent of the prints that ordinarily just couldn't make it. Is your print coming up normally, but contrast? Put it in the 100F water for one or two seconds and then continue developing. The whites will jump up full of detail and your print will have softer contrast. Given this "liquid hot foot" most other papers will fog: they just can't take it.

"Bleach" It. (Potassium Ferricyanide)

This chemical is invaluable for clearing highlights, increasing contrast or brightening muddy, over burned-in whites. It can also be used for lightening faces, hands, or backgrounds which are too dark.

Unlike some papers, Varigam normally will not stain from the ferricyanide when processed in a fixing bath with hardener. To prepare the ferricyanide solution use about 16 oz. of cold water (temperature is not important) in an 8x10 tray and sprinkle enough potassium ferricyanide to produce the color of a K2 (medium yellow) filter. For more stubborn areas make a solution of three ounces in a 5x7 tray with about the same amount of ferricyanide as was used in the 8x10 tray. Tilt this tray so one end is dry and for very stubborn areas, sprinkle a little ferricyanide on the dry end. Work a bit of this dry ferricyanide into a wet brush. You now have the strongest solution you can use. Your fingers and palm are the best applicators for larger areas; use a No. 4 spotting brush for smaller ones. Take the print out of hypo, treat it with bleaching solution, and put the print back in hypo. If the whole print needs brightening, dunk it for two or three seconds in the 8x10 tray solution, then swish it in plain water (not essential—just to avoid unnecessary amounts of ferricyanide from getting into hypo) and throw it into the hypo to stop the bleaching action. Result: More prints saved or improved with a treatment that would make many papers blanch and run for the waste basket. "Broil" it? I've never thought to, but I'll try it, thank you. Trust Varigam to produce some beneficial result.

Other Advantages of Varigam

a. DuPont Varigam is fast. Without a filter it has about the speed and contrast of DuPont Velour Black No. 2. Filters 4, 5 and 6 will cut the speed in half; the others a little more. For very dense negatives there is still faster Varigam High Speed.

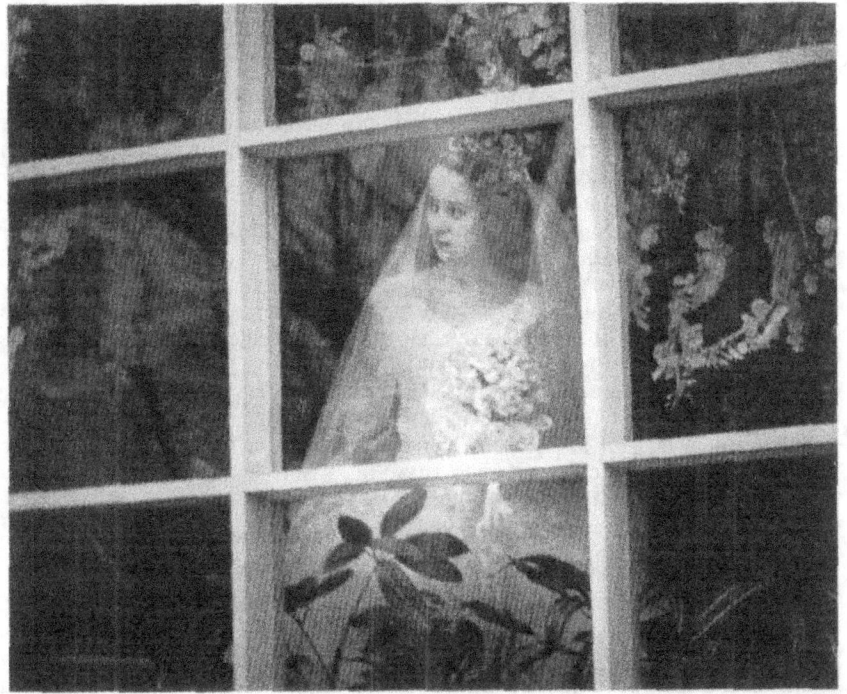

51. *Available light provides the opportunity for many other imaginative photos. This was taken on a cloudy day from outside the window. It was deliberately made from a distance of 20 feet so that only a portion of the negative would be used and the grain thereby emphasized. The strong white lines which provide the framing were further brightened on the print by ferricyanide. The outside edges of the print are slightly burned in. (Mamiya 6; Tri-X; 1/50 second, f/5.6; film developed in Microdol.)*

    b. All your paper supply is in one box instead of four.

    c. Through the use of filters, (or the Simmon-Omega Electronic Variable Contrast Timer, an automatic device) No. 1 to No. 4 paper contrasts or a combination of these contrasts can be achieved on one sheet of paper.

    d. Developers recommended by DuPont or other paper developers will work. (I use Kodak's Dektol, 1:2.)

    e. The DL surface is a good choice, and will accept work with etching knife or razor blade.

    f. Varigam can withstand considerable handling during development without getting fingerprint stains.

No—variable contrast paper is not an eccentric, but as stable and down-to-earth as the conventional graded ones. Its basic rules: reach for a filter instead of a grade of paper; use the harder {higher number) filter first when two or more are employed; use an opal enlarging lamp, or the one whose color temperature approximates it. Varigain is related to all papers by its need for reasonable observance of the manufacturer's recommendations as to developer temperature and length of development.

I do not believe warm-tone papers are necessary when faces are mostly the size of a fingernail. For those who prefer a variable contrast paper with a warm tone, DuPont makes Varilour. But there is a catch. Varilour is not the paper Varigam is: Varilour can't take it. . . .

Eastman's Kodabromide, Ansco's Brovira, DuPont's Velour Black, or any paper with four or five contrasts will turn out good candids. But with the incomparable Varigam in your easel and a magic filter in your hand, you are ready to conjure delicate contrasts onto your print—contrasts that until now you never hoped to reproduce with your negatives.

Demon Dust

Dust can mean many things to many people. To the 8x10 contact worker, dust is no cause for concern. The 4x5 film user will admit his prints need a little spotting. The 2¼x2¼ man is ready to agree dust is a problem; that spotting consumes a large portion of his print-making time. The 35mm addict is best left alone or he may forget he's a gentleman. I've fought Demon Dust for many years. Experience has made me a worthy adversary. Here are the weapons I use to keep Demon Dust in his place. With these weapons the print from a 35mm negative will need little more spotting than one from a 4x5.

1. Before starting to work I wipe my enlarging table with a damp towel.

2. If humidity is low and static electricity high, I steam my darkroom every half hour by turning on the hot water faucet for several minutes. (A vaporizer will do as well.)

3. First, I squeegee the film through my index and middle finger to dis lodge the dust, then brush it with a static neutralizing brush. Finally, I attack the minute but stubborn particles with a blast of air from the exhaust of an old vacuum cleaner. (I use the rubber narrow-slitted "crevice tool" attachment to

52. Posing the couple at the piano is a variation of the usual formal pose, and the mirror adds interest. (Rolleiflex; Tri-X; 80 w/s electronic flash, 1/250, f/11; Microdol.) 53, 54, 55. The other three pictures (opposite) indicate the possibilities of synchro-sunlight for formal and semi-formal photos. (Upper right: Minolta Autocord; Tri-X; 80 w/s unit, 1/200, f/11. Lower left: Rolleiflex; Tri-X; 80 w/s unit, 1/250, f/16. Lower right: Busch Pressman; Tri-X; 80 w/s unit, 1/190, f/16.)

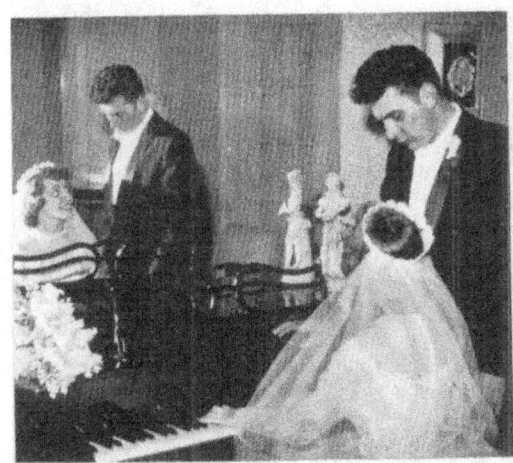
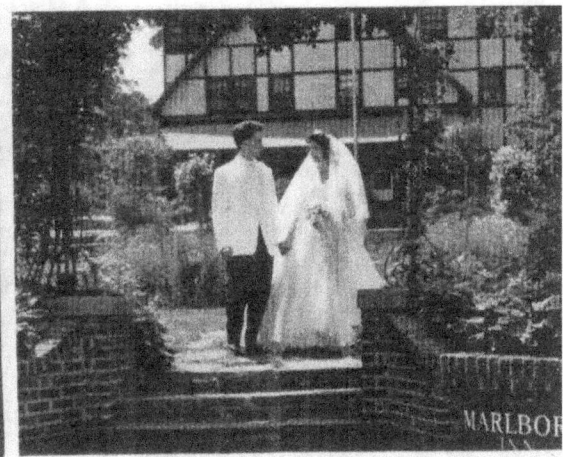
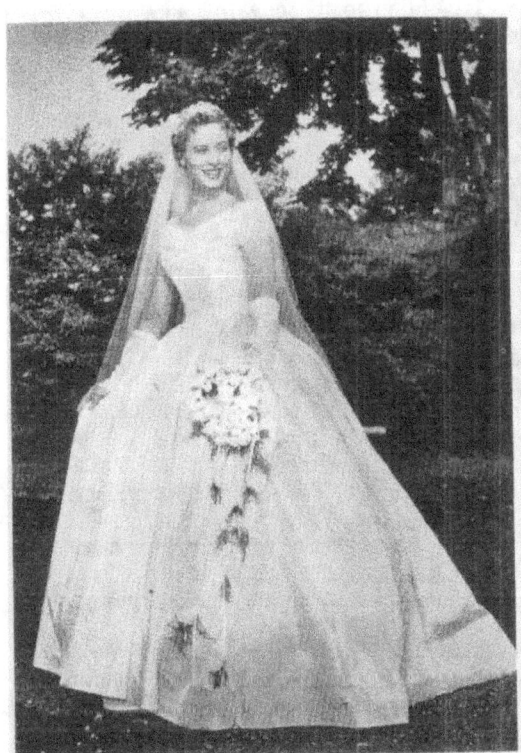
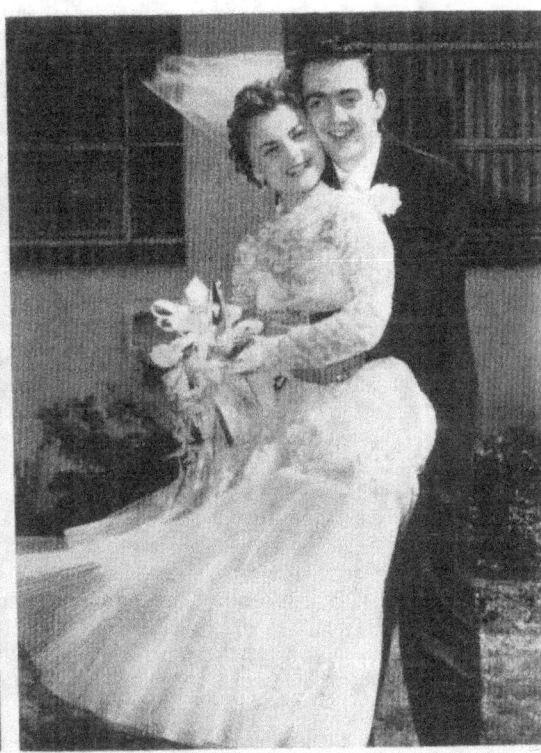

increase the force of air.) The vacuum cleaner stands about a foot from the floor. To filter the dust and add to the humidity, a heavy turkish towel soaked and wrung out is hung about three or four inches in front of the intake hole.

4. A wire leading from a metal part of my enlarger to a water pipe or radiator acts as a ground and dissipates any static electricity I create through friction.

5. And, of course, I occasionally mop the darkroom floor.

These are the weapons I use. But what about those beautiful negatives that at best make only a gray print? Is the paper manufacturer slipping? Not by a long shot! How long has it been since you cleaned your Varigam filters, enlarger condensers, or the top of your lens? Take them out and look at them. Shocked? Clean them and your world will be bright again and Demon Dust, if only for the moment, will be brought to heel.

Darkrooth Aids for a Better Candid

Several other darkroom aids will come in handy—one is for improving the difficult negative; another for saving the under-exposed film; the last two for cutting washing time.

New Coccine (Ansco): This dye is applied to the negative in order to brighten highlights in the hair, and to hands to prevent them from going dark when burning-in gown, bouquet or white dinner jackets. It can also be used to reduce contrast by holding back dark areas.

Victor Intensifter: To build up density and contrast in weak, flat negatives. Note: Intensifies only add density where some detail already exists in the negative. If they are used with small negative sizes, grainy looking enlargements are likely to result.

Kodalk: A 2 percent solution cuts washing time in half.

BF No. 30; A 10 percent solution cuts washing time 75 percent.

Retouching

The ability to retouch is of particular importance to the candid wedding photographer. True, extensive retouching is not needed on most candid photos, but there is no excuse for pimples, missing or recessed teeth. For all practical purposes retouching the small heads of the full-length figures is difficult on the 4x5 and roll film negatives and next to impossible with the 35mm sizes. Removing blemishes on the print by bleaching is time consuming and not feasible with candids where one order can mean as many as fifty or more pictures.

The only rapid method is to work on the dry print with knife or razor blade, dye or spotting material, brushes and pencil. Several seconds with a blade can remove a pimple; within a minute or two a tooth can be repaired. Hair lines can be filled-in or stray hair etched out.

I prefer the double edge razor blade broken in half, then the halves broken in two. Use the broken and not the rounded edge. Sharpening an etching knife is an art in itself and besides I feel Gillette can do it better.

There is not much to be said on how to etch except to keep the edge of the blade almost flat to the surface and shave lightly. What we are really doing is erasing with a razor blade. Do not dig. Good etching should be such that little or no spotting is needed when you are through. For very small black spots use the point of the blade. It is not hard to get the knack. With a little patience and practice the "feel" will come.

For spotting, the 00 sable brush is necessary. (Windsor and Newton is a fine make.) I prefer the liquid Spotone No. 3 for photo-finishing and spotting. It can be diluted to any shade you need, and being a dye leaves no surface deposit. Use a feathery stippling motion with your brush for smaller areas—a feathery stroking or circular motion for larger ones. A damp finger patted on the spotting will diffuse and tie it together. A damp finger patted on a stubborn area will make it more receptive to the spotting dye. Small spots that received too much dye can be lightened by rubbing with the wet wooden end of the brush.

The dye can be applied directly from bottle cap to brush and spotting done first on the dark areas working up to grey and white portions of the print as the dye on the brush becomes lighter through lip moistening. This is the method I use. Another method is to prepare three little bottle caps, the first with two drops of undiluted dye, in the second dye diluted 1:3, and in the third 1:5. Use two brushes, keeping one for the full strength dye. Work with the dye lighter than the area surrounding the spot and build-up density.

A 9H retouching lead can be used for filling-in small spots on lighter areas. Spot, then rub with your finger. After two or three attempts the spotting will be there to stay.

As with etching, the principles of application are simple but the knack can be acquired only through practice.

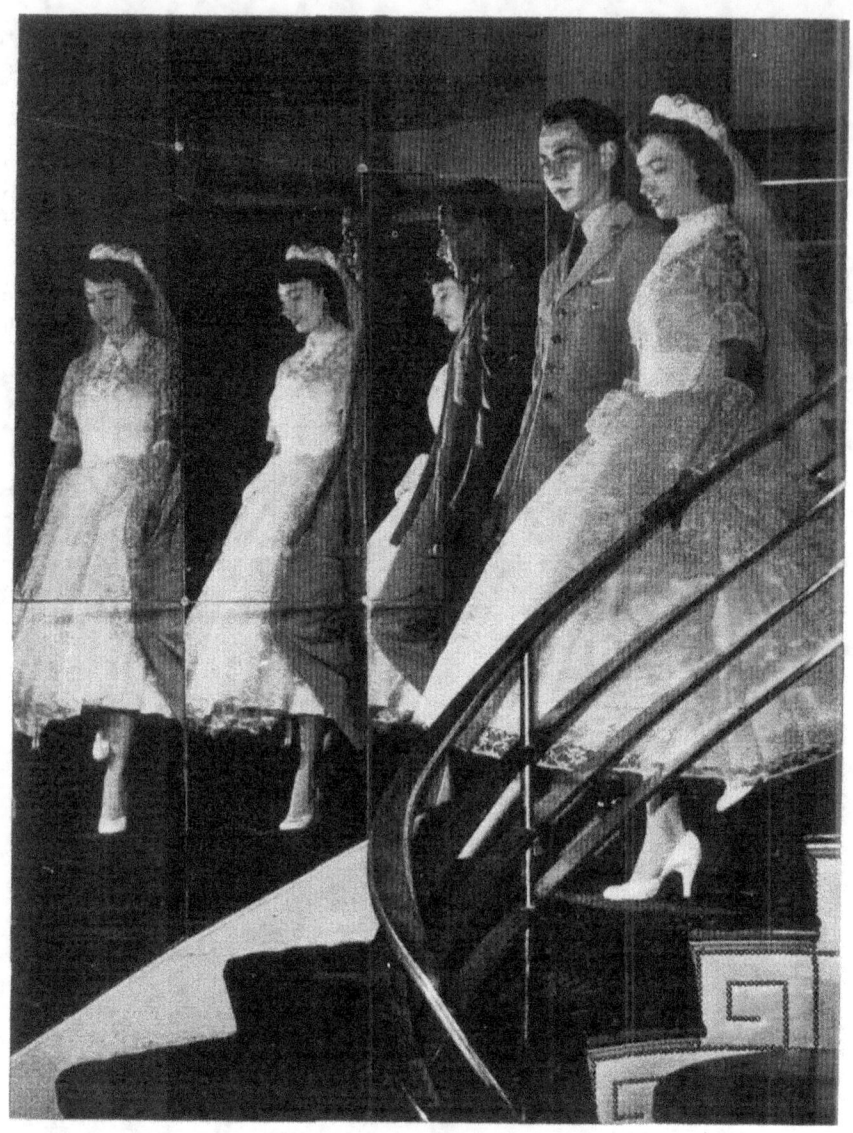

56. *This couple was posed on the stairs as they entered the reception because an opportunity like this sectional mirror does not often occur. As with all mirror shots try to stop down sufficiently so both the subject and the mirror image are in focus. (Rolleiflex; Verichrome Pan; 80 w/s electronic flash unit, 1/250 second, f/8; film developed in D-76.)*

11.

Color-2D and 3D

TODAY COLOR, the stereo candid, is vying for popularity with black and white. In many instances, the bridal couple decide to have 3D color as well as an album. By being able to shoot both, the photographer can add substantially to his income.

Much that you know about black-and-white can be applied to color. But, unlike black-and-white, there is no remedy for faulty composition or any practical remedy for incorrect exposures. You will get exactly what you shoot. Even if you do your own processing, any liberties taken with development will affect the general color balance and specifically the fleshtones. Good fleshtones are an important consideration with a 3D candid. The best results can be obtained by following the rules laid down by the manufacturer.

Film

From the standpoint of economy, it does not pay, either in time or material, to process only one or two weddings in color a week. Eastman Kodak (the most popular film company with wedding photographers) offers four 35mm color films that can be used for 3D candids. Kodachrome Type F and Ektachrome Type F (both balanced for clear, M Type, No. 5 and 25 bulbs), Kodachrome Daylight and Ektachrome Daylight. Kodak also provides stereo-mounting and a 20-exposure (15 stereo pair) magazine, or a 36-exposure (28 stereo pair) magazine—in Kodachrome only. Kodachrome Professional Film, Type A, is color-balanced for photo-flood use and requires an 81C filter for M-Type flash. With the filter it is one-half an f/stop slower than Kodachrome, Type F. It offers no advantage for flash use.

Ansco offers 35 mm Anscochrome Flash (balanced for clear, M Type No. 5 and 25 bulbs) and Anscochrome (daylight). Ansco also maintains a stereo mounting service. At present the 20 exposure roll is the only length packaged by Ansco. Anscochrome has the same speed (film speed: 32) as Ektachrome Daylight. Anscochrome Flash and Ektachrome Type F have just about the same guide numbers. The new super-speed Anscochrome is rated at 100 and may be exposed at somewhat higher speeds. However, none approaches the grainlessness that is possible with Kodachrome.

There are four reasons that influence the candid wedding photographer to favor Kodachrome. *First,* most candid wedding customers seem to prefer the color quality of Kodachrome. *Second,* Ansco offers no counterpart to the ultrafme-grain Kodachrome. *Third,* the Kodachrome 36-exposure roll minimizes film changes. (With two magazines you can cover a wedding.) *Fourth,* with a No. 5 or 25 bulb, Kodachrome, Type F is fast enough to cover any indoor shot in a 3D candid wedding. The first two are the important reasons for my preference of Kodachrome film for stereo use; the more important of these two is Kodachrome's quality.

Ektachrome is not processed by Kodak, but by independent laboratories, or by yourself. Anscochrome can be processed by yourself, by independent laboratories, or mailed directly to Ansco. Kodachrome is processed both by Kodak and independent laboratories.

Straight Flash with Bulbs

One guide number is adequate for all black-and-white exposures with a particular film-flashbulb-shutter speed combination. Contrast can be controlled during film development or through paper grade. But color photographs, normally processed, depend wholly on exposure. So for good flash results, we need three color guide numbers for each film. All listed are for taking either 35mm or 3D color pictures. Remember that 1/25 second is the highest flashbulb synchronization speed for most stereo cameras.

3D, 35MM SLIDES, AND KODACOLOB

(For use with No. 5 or 25 bulbs at 1/25 sec; or with FP6 or 26 focal-plane bulbs at 1/50 sec) °

GROUP	KOPA-CHROME TYPE F	EKTA-CHHOME TYPE F OR KODACOLOR	ANSCO-CHROME FLASH	KODACOLOR No. 5 or 25 at 1/50	No. 5 or 25 at 1/100	No. 6 or 26 at 1/50
1. Small room (about 8x11)	115	150	160	140	115	150
2. Average room (about 14x18)	105	135	140	125	105	135
3. Church, reception hall, or any large, high-ceil-inged room.*[10]	95	120	125	110	95	120

° With 4-5 inch polished reflector; with satin finish, open ½ stop.

°° For exposures in Group 3 that are 12 feet or closer, use Group 2 guide numbers.

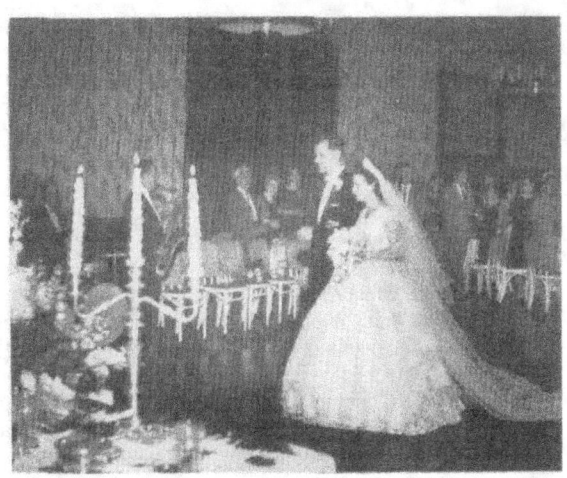

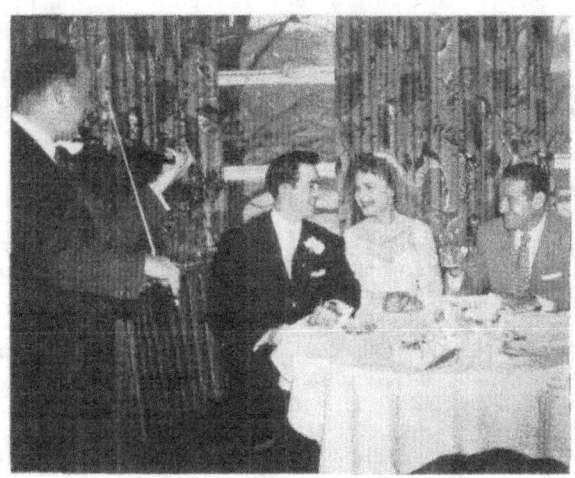

57. *This view of the couple concentrates attention on them as they enter the reception hall. (Compare with picture 59, page 99). If you include a large bridal party as it enters, focus on the couple—they judge the sharpness of the photo by their own faces—but aim your flashgun and set your f/stop for a point half-way between the first and last couples. (Rolleiflex; Tri-X; 135 w/s unit, 1/250, f/11; Microdol.)* 58. *A shot such as this (left) of the couple being serenaded is romantic and intimate and is a priceless addition to bridal album. If your flash unit is strong enough, use partial bounce. (Busch Press-mann; Tri-X; 60 w/s unit, 1/200, f/8; developed in DK-50.)*

The photographer using a between-the-lens or behind-the-lens fully synchronized shutter and a No. 5 or 25 bulb, might prefer to work with a faster shutter speed. With Ektachrorne Type F or Anscochrome Flash, use the guide numbers under 1/100 in the Kodacolor section of the chart. For Kodachrome Type F, reduce the guide number by 20%.

If you don't have this chart handy when you shoot, look at the instruction sheet which comes with your film and modify the manufacturer's recommendations as follows: In large rooms, use the guide number recommended by the manufacturer for average subjects; in average size rooms, close down ¼ stop more, and in small rooms, ½ stop more than for average subjects.

This rule, or the table of guide numbers, will serve as a springboard to good color. In time, you will find yourself further refining or making compromise exposures, as in the case of overexposing a light-skinned bride slightly, to improve the rendition of the skin color of a sun-tanned groom.

Color and Electronic Flash

Since the light from many electronic flash tubes is slightly bluer than the light for which Daylight Type color films are balanced, you may need to use a correction filter. With Anscochrome Daylight Film Ansco recommends an 81A filter. For Kodak daylight color films consult the manufacturer of your electronic flash unit. Now, some background information: the color of the light produced by your electronic flash, and the color of the light for which a specific color film is balanced, are both measured in degrees Kelvin (K). The higher the number, the bluer the light. The degrees Kelvin (or color temperature) of the light emitted by your electronic flash unit should be almost the same as the degrees Kelvin for which daylight color film is balanced. It's when the two color temperatures are slightly different that you need a correction filter which changes the color temperature of your flash before it reaches the film. No filter is needed when electronic flash is used for synchro-sunlight.

With that clarified, how powerful must your unit be for color, and what can you expect of some of the units already discussed for black-and-white use? Ektachrome or Anscochrome Daylight Type, with a film speed rating of 32, can be used with the more powerful electronic flash units. First of all, none of the units we've used for black-and-white is strong enough. A comfortable working guide number for the candid wedding photographer is somewhere between 85 and 100. Over 100 would be better, and the same unit could be used for black and white if it had three position power control for half power and quarter (or a third) power. But I'll let you in on a secret: you'll be loaded with some 12-pounds.

But back to the color guide numbers for some of the units which I use successfully in black-and-white work (see Chapter 4). There's no use even talking about a 60-watt-second unit for color film and candid wedding photography. Even an 80-watt-second electronic flash will only give you a color guide number of 50 at most. The Ultra blitz Matador I with 135-watt-second input is tremendous for black and white, but it only dents my color film. To record good flesh tones in a room of average size and height, (with white ceiling) I could only use a color guide number of 60-65.

So, if you have the strength of a pack horse, and are willing to call portable equipment with the weight of a studio unit, try working in color with a

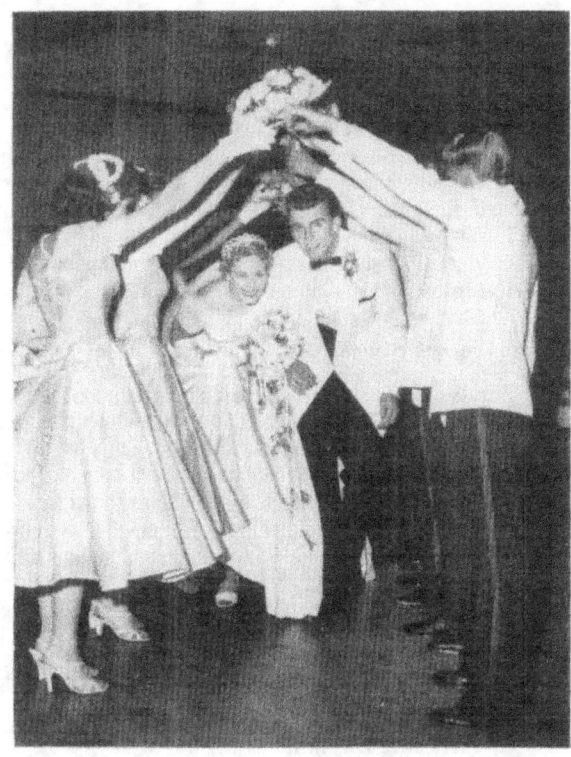

59. *Occasionally you will encounter an unusual entrance of the bridal couple to the reception hall. This will become a novelty which you can introduce into future weddings. (Rolleiflex; Tri-X; 80 w/s electronic -flash, 1/250, f/lQ; Microdol.)*

unit that has at least a 200-watt-second input. If not, do as I do, use flashbulbs for all 3D and 2D color work. Everytime I fill my pockets with flashbulbs I add a silent blessing to that little bulb of glass which gives me a comfortable guide number and fine color results.

While we've been talking about color and electronic flash, there has been a weak but persistent voice from the peanut gallery. "What about *Super Anscochrome?*" OK, what about it? Super Anscochrome *with electronic flash?* Have I tried it? Yes! Let's take a look at the facts, magnified. In color characteristics Super Anscochrome can be compared with regular Anscochrome. Exposing for the flesh tones and in the average-sized room, my tests established a guide number of 150 with my "Matador I" (135 w/s) unit at full power. The recommended 81A filter was used. An 80 w/s unit should give a guide number of about 90. This is potent stuff, but not for us.

In a hand viewer, 3D slides show obvious grain; with 35mm slides projected, the grain is still there but not so apparent. With 2¼x2¼ or Super-Slides (38x38mm) you *might* get away with it—but not if the bridal couple have seen Kodachrome. To sum it up, forget it. Super Anscochrome is a most welcome addition to the family of color films but not for candid weddings.

Color and Synchro-Sunlight

For synchro-sunlight with color film, both the first rule and the second rule apply just as they do in black-and-white photography. (See Chapter 5 on Synchro-Sunlight for complete details). Only two things will be different than for black-and-white: the basic sunlight exposure of your color film which can be determined as described in the next paragraph, and your color guide number. The chart following gives guide numbers for synchro-sunlight with color film and flashbulb. If you're using an electronic flash unit, find your guide number by running the test described in Chapter 4, Flash and Electronic Flash.

No meter is needed to determine the basic sunlight exposure, for a subject facing the sun. With *all* color films place the number "1" over the exposure index (film speed), to find the shutter speed to use at f/16. Sunlight exposures at 1/25 are:

Kodachrome Type F (film speed: 10 with 85C filter); f/10.
Kodachrome Daylight (film speed: 10) f/10.
Ektachrome Type F (film speed: 20 with 85C filter) f/14.
Ektachrome Daylight (film speed: 32) f/19.
Anscochrome (film speed: 32) f/19.
Anscochrome Flash Type (film speed: 25 with 85C filter) f/16.

All recommended settings are basic exposures (average), intended to encompass the extremes of black-and-white clothing. In the case of a fair-skinned bride or groom, one-half stop smaller lens opening will improve both flesh-tones, and detail in a light-colored gown. With open shade, open up three f/stops more than for the basic sunlight exposure. For other conditions, use an exposure meter.

Conversion Filters

Some candid wedding photographers find it easier to rely on one color film for both indoor and outdoor flashbulb shots—hence they need only one color camera. Of course it's safer to take two. They use a Type F film, as is, for indoor flashbulb shots. Outdoors they add the appropriate conversion filter. The 85C filter will convert Type F film (Kodachrome, Ektachrome or Anseo-chrome Flash) to outdoor use. With Kodachrome Type F it will produce the pleasantly warm quality that is similar to the results obtained with Kodachrome Daylight film and Skylight (1A) filter, or that is "normal" for Ektachrome film without a filter. Kodachrome Type F converted to daylight is rated at 10—the same as Kodachrome Daylight. Ektachrome Type F converted has a daylight rating of 20; Anscochrome Flash Type, 25.

SYNCHRO-SUNLIGHT GUIDE NUMBERS FOR USE WITH COLOR FILM
(use at speeds marked, with polished reflectors * of sizes indicated)

BLUE FLASHBULBS

FILM	5B 1/25 sec. 4-6-in. reflector	22B 1/25 sec. 6-7 in. reflector	50B 1/25 sec. med. size studio reflector	FP6B 1/100 sec. 4-5 in. reflector	FP31B 1/25 sec. 6-7 in. reflector
Kodachrome, Type F (with 85C filter)	60	80	120	32	85
Kodachrome, Daylight	60	80	120	32	85
Ektachrome, Type F (with 85C filter)	85	120	170	44	120
Anscochrome Flash Type (with 85C filter)	95	130	190	50	140
Anscochrome and Ektachrome, Daylight (Index, 32)	110	150	220	55	160
Kodacolor	110	150	220	55	160

CLEAR FLASHBULBS **

FILM	5 1/25 sec. 4-6 in. reflector	22 1/25 sec. 6-7 in. reflector	50 1/25 sec. med. size studio reflector	FP6 1/100 sec. 4-6 in. reflector	FP31 1/25 sec. 6-7 in. reflector
Kodachrome, Type F (with 85C filter)	85	120	170	46	130
Kodachrome, Daylight	85	120	170	46	130
Ektachrome, Type F (with 85C filter)	120	170	240	65	180
Anscochrome Flash Type (with 85C filter)	140	190	280	75	200
Anscochrome and Ektachrome, Daylight (Index, 32)	160	220	320	85	220
Kodacolor	Clear flashbulbs not recommended for synchro-sunlight				

* In straight flash, guide numbers for satin-finish reflectors are slightly lower than those for polished reflectors. However, you can use satin-finish reflectors with the guide numbers given above, because the quality of your synchro-sun picture is based on sun. The bulb merely acts as fill-in.

** Although blue bulbs are recommended for daylight color film (transparencies), many photographers prefer the warm tones of a clear bulb for synchro-sunlight. My opinion is that the clear bulbs give fleshtones a healthier look.

The only dubious advantage which Anscochrome Flash Type or Ekta-chrome Type F offers over Kodachrome Type F in flash candids is a little more than half an f/'stop in speed. But, a fast shutter speed can not be used, as most of today's stereo cameras are synchronized only up to 1/25 second for Class M flashbulbs.

In the colder months, the S5C conversion filter can be used with Type F films for the five or six outdoor shots- In the milder months, this conversion will yield excellent results until about five o'clock Daylight Saving Time. If the outdoor shots arc to be taken after five, it would pay to load the second camera with a twenty exposure (15 stereo pair) Daylight roll. The results will be warm, but not so warm-toned as with converted Type F film.

Trying to correct the late afternoon, golden fieshtones by filter is not feasible. Any filter used to make warm fieshtones colder will also make bluer the shadow areas that are illuminated, not by the sun but by reflected blue skylight. The bridal couple seldom objects to the warm fieshtones when the reason is explained. If you want to play it safe, shoot the bridal formals indoors as well as outdoors.

General Shooting Tips

Blue flashbulbs with daylight film offer no advantage for indoor shooting. If you are going to use flashbulbs, Kodachrome or Ektachrome Type F, or Anscochrome Flash with No. 5 or No. 25 (cheaper than blue bulbs) are by far, better combinations. They provide a higher guide number and produce superior color.

Bounce-light in unfamiliar surroundings is not to be trusted with color. Even white may not be white, but contain colors the eye does not perceive. The light will transmit the hue of the walls and ceiling, and may distort the coloring of the subjects, most noticeably in the fleshtones.

Use of sunlight with the bridal party, or as a general rule with full-length pictures of the couple, should be kept simple—front or at most, three-quarter. Even with frontlighting the height of the sun will provide enough modeling. Pictures of the bride alone need no restriction. Side and backlighting produce dramatic results, but unless silhouette or semi-silhouettes are intended, the fill-in, (especially with backlight) has to be accurate. Backlighting with bride and groom, particularly on closer informal poses can be as dramatic as those of the bride alone. As a blow-up is not possible with the usual 3D viewer, take one or two backlighted shots from as close as five feet. With the sun facing your lens, be sure to use a lens-shade.

Soft and beautiful effects can be attained on clear sunny days by shooting in the open shade (unobstructed sky over subject). The color reaching your subject is reflection from the blue sky and a Skylight filter (1A) is needed for Kodachrome and Ektachrome Daylight or Anscochrome to warm this excess of blue. The Skylight filter requires no change in exposure. Type F film converted to daylight needs no added filter as the 85C has the ultra-violet absorption properties of the Skylight filter. The same holds true on clear days when the sun is obscured by an occasional cloud. For open shade, open the lens diaphragm three f/stops from the basic sunlight exposure.

On overcast but bright days, the Skylight filter is again necessary with daylight film. With Type F, the 85C is all you need. If the sun should come

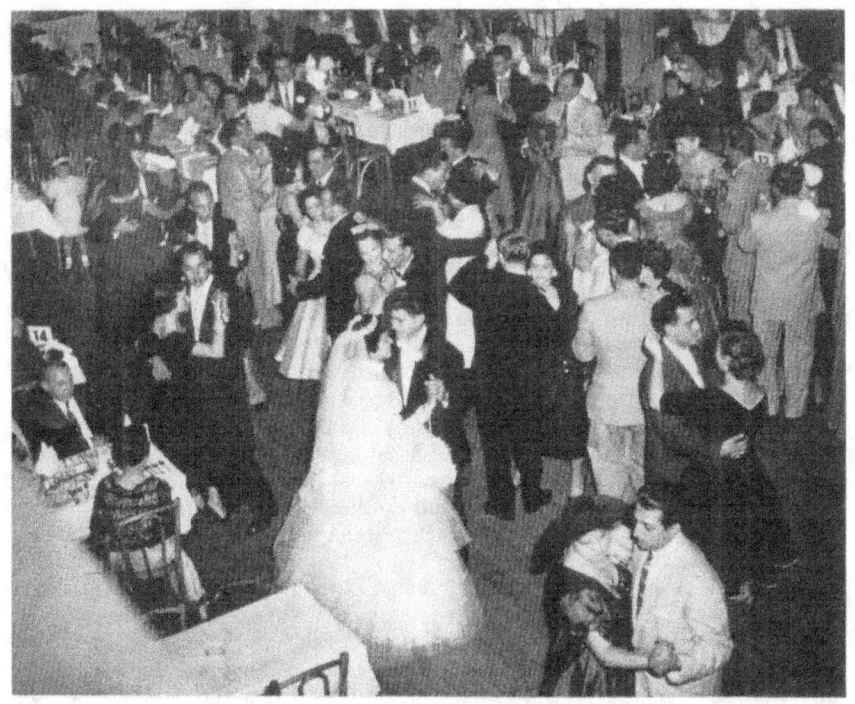

60. *There is no set time for dancing at the reception. It may start right away or not until later. It is best to shoot the dancing couple at a distance of about 15 feet. If possible, keep them close to the bandstand so that the musicians may be seen, and also try to include other dancing couples. In a small hall, set the f/stop for your flash exposure for the distance to the couple; in a larger hall over-expose them one-half stop in order to get more detail in the background. Normally, only one person's face will show while a couple dances, so ask them both to look in one direction. Other possible pictures include the bride dancing with her father or father-in-law and the groom with his mother or mother-in-law. If you are restricted, however, to 50 or 60 shots, there is a limit to how many dancing shots you can make. In the picture above, I took advantage of the balcony to show the size of the hall and the number of guests. The flash reflector was aimed at the people farthest away. When the print was made, the Varigam paper was first exposed through a No. 8 filter to bring out detail in the most distant areas, then the couple was given additional exposure with no filter. (Minolta Autocord; Tri-X; GO w/s electronic flash unit, 1/200, f/3.5; developed in Microdol.)*

out and you're using Kodachrome daylight film, leave the Skylight filter, on. The results will be warmer but pleasant. Ektachrome and Anscochrome daylight films are inherently warmer so it is best to take the Skylight filter off.

For any other than a sunny day or open shade situation where exposures are constant, the use of an accurate light meter is essential; especially if a flash fill-in is used. With a reflected-light meter, take the reading off the palm of your hand; with an incident-light meter, take it from subject position and aim the meter's light gathering cell at your camera.

About what film to use, it all breaks down to this:

1. If you are familiar with Kodachrome and do not need the speed of Ektachrome or Anscochrome (and you do not, other than with electronic flash)—stick to Kodachrome. Its color quality is by far the best.

2. If you feel the need for additional depth of field for your 3D color flash shots (one-half stop), or would like to eliminate the waiting period for processing, use Ektachrome or Anscochrome and process it yourself.

3. If your electronic flash unit can produce a guide number of 85 or better with Anscochrome or Ektachrome Daylight you can shoot a candid wedding with these films. The benefits are many: home or commercial processing; a substantial savings on flashbulbs; action-stopping flash; no need for conversion filter; added film speed for in-the-shade or cloudy-day exposures.

The temptations are enough to try the faith of Type F Kodachrome clear-bulb converts. Many will hang that 12-pound or more electronic flash unit from their shoulders. But in the end, it's results that count. What they will find with electronic flash is:

a. Anscochrome has a reddish overcast, and despite the use of the recommended filter, there is a general color distortion, highlights become purplish, faces take on a reddish hue.

b. Ektachrome is superior to Anscochrome in color fidelity, noticed most in the fleshtones. But all color film has a relatively narrow latitude in exposure.

c. At the end of experiments many will conclude that compared to Type F Kodachrome and clear-bulb, electronic flash with Anscochrome can be rated, at best, acceptable, and Ektachrome, quite good.

Once again, many of our experimenters will come back into the fold-filling their pockets with No. 5's, and their cameras with the unmatchable Kodachrome Type F.

Kodachrome Type F, Kodachrome Daylight, Ektachrome Type F, Ektachrome Daylight, Anscochrome and Anscochrome Flash—all are superb tools with which to work. For candids, the choice of one film over another boils down to a matter of personal preference. For the average bridal couple color transparencies professionally exposed are wonderful. *Wonderful* in Kodachrome! *Wonderful* in Ektachrome! *Wonderful* in Anscochrome! The 36 exposure (28 stereo pair) roll will take you through the house and church. Two magazines normally are enough for the whole wedding.

Which Camera for 3D?

The Revere Stereo and the Stereo Realist are the cameras used by almost all professionals. They are well-designed, well-finished, devoid of mechanical bugs, and have coupled rangefinders. I prefer the Revere. With this camera, the shutter is automatically cocked as the film is advanced. With the Realist

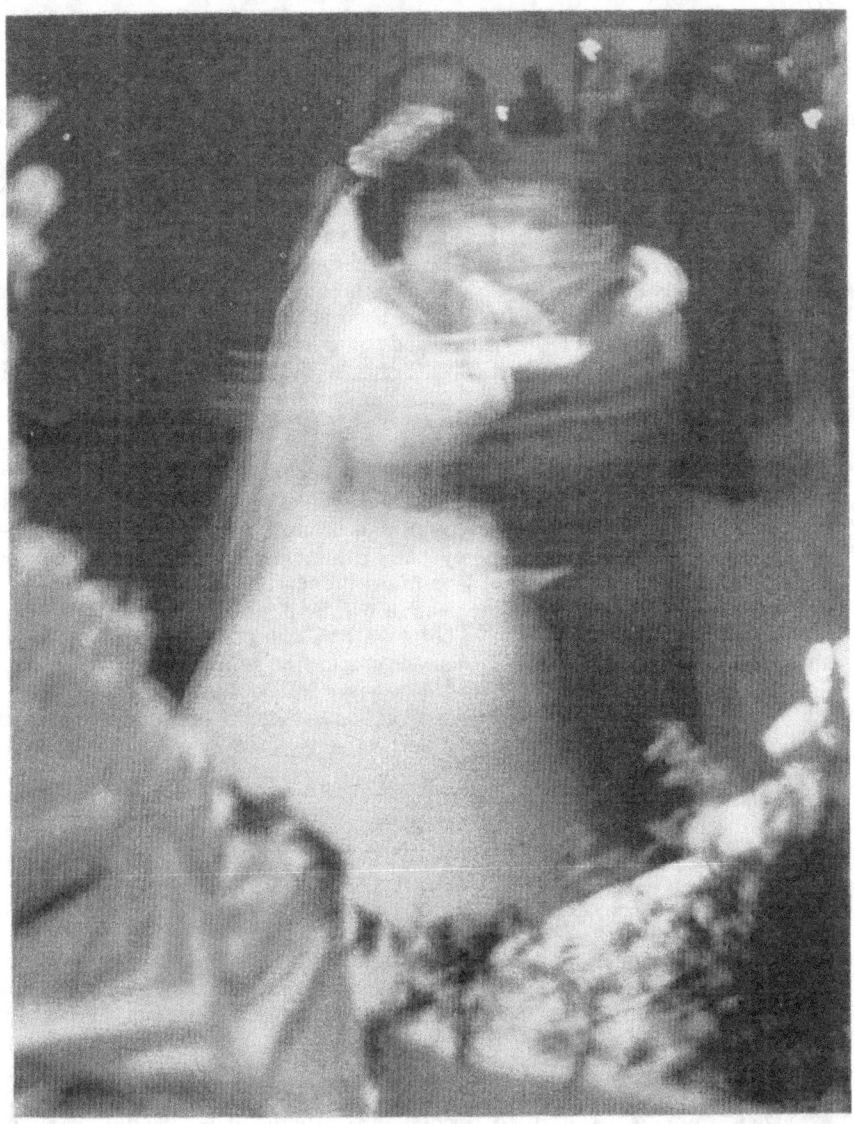

61. Here is a dancing picture which is off the beaten track and will be appreciated by clients who like "something different." Exposure on Tri-X was 1/8 second at f/4 with light from 60 w/s electronic flash bounced from the ceiling. (Rolleiflex camera.)

the shutter is cocked manually. The Revere is equipped with an f/3.5 lens and a 1/2 to 1/200 sec, T&B shutter. There is also the Wollensak Stereo "10" (Wollensak is a subsidiary of Revere). It is identical with the Revere in design and operation, but has a top speed of 1/300, and f/2.7 lenses. The Realist has two models, the ST-41 with f/3.5 lenses and a 1 sec. to 1/150 T&B shutter and the ST-42 with f/2.8 lenses and 1 sec. to 1/200 shutter. The f/3.5 is fast enough with flashbulbs; the f/2.8 should be the choice with electronic flash. The rangefinder is as essential for establishing the number of feet from camera to subject so that the guide number can be used accurately as it is for attaining picture sharpness. The TDC Stereo Vivid camera has a desirable feature. After an adjustment is made for a particular flashbulb, the f/stop is automatically set with each change of focus.

Special Problems

"Pink Eye" occurs in color when the flashgun is close to, or on the camera. The light travels through the eye pupil and then is reflected by the reddish retina (back wall of eye) onto the eyeball. The incidence of "pink eye" can be minimized by moving the gun 8 or more inches to one side or above the camera. Having the gun above the camera will help hide the subject's shadow.

There is just one limitation to color—a bad skin condition. In these cases suggest a black and white album. Panchromatic film will do most of the trick aided by photo-retouching.

It might be mentioned that 3D photographs should be quite sharp from foreground to background. Most of our focusing is beyond 10 feet, and the depth of field of the usual 35mm lens of a 3D camera is tremendous. With a combination like this, how can we miss.

In the first paragraph I mentioned that the bridal couple often decide on both black and white and 3D color. It has been common practice to mount the stereo camera on the press camera with a Candid Stereo Bracket—or with a homemade version—and by means of this accessory expose black and white and color simultaneously with the same flashbulb. This practice is dishonest unless the couple have been told that both films will be identical in action and expression. If the bride and groom are paying for two jobs they are entitled to a conscientious effort on the part of the photographer to avoid exact duplication. Sooner or later, they will see other couples' pictures in which the black and white and color differ and they will feel they have been cheated. In the long run, it is the photographer who is cheated. Recommendations can not be expected from a disgruntled bride and groom. The candid wedding photographer's step ladder to success is satisfied couples.

If you do not feel capable of shooting both stereo and black and white by yourself, hire a photographer to assist you with either of the jobs. The cost incurred, in shooting 3D separately, will be more than overcome. By eliminating duplication you give the couple more pictures from which to select and give yourself a larger order.

The Sad Case of 2D Color

Before we leave color, I'd like to remark on the role (or lack of it) which 2D, 35mm color occupies in candid wedding photography. The rave is all 3D color and there is almost no call for 35mrn color slides. Perhaps this is because 35mm photographers have not exploited this "natural" in wedding photography.

For those of you who want to explore the 2D possibilities, we contrast stereo viewing equipment with that available for 2D color. We also give suggested 2D prices. Both points should provide selling arguments. With stereo candids, unfortunately the bride and groom's viewing in 3D is generally limited by price to an AC, or battery-operated, eye viewer. For the couple whose interest in 3D does not usually extend beyond the photos of their wedding, stereo projectors are prohibitively expensive. They range from $75 to $200. However, 3D slides can be viewed (though in 2D) with 35mm projectors. Some units are designed to accommodate the slide and show a single frame of the stereo pair; for others you need a special attachment.

With 35mm, 2D color slides the situation is different, and the advantages are:

1. Hand viewers can be had for as little as $2, and with small inex pensive table viewers, viewing is possible by more than one person at the same time. A good projector is available for only $35 to $60.

2. The bride and groom can add other color slides with a 35mm camera that also can be used for black-and-white snapshots.

3. Little or no grain for all normal purposes.

Pricing for 2D, 35mm color can be at the rate of three dollars per slide plus your charge for the viewer selected. I would suggest twenty slides as a minimum order. As with 3D assignments, also take black-and-white shots of the bride, bride and groom, bridal party, and parents with the couple. A reasonable charge is three dollars for an 8x10 with folder.

Remember, the exposure data for 3D color can be applied in its entirety to 35mm 2D color slides.

Color Prints

Color transparencies for projection, and 3D color with its true-to-life qualities, have done much to satisfy some of the demand for pictures in "natural color." A candid wedding in color transparencies is within the public's financial reach.

Kodak's Kodacolor Film Universal Type (for daylight and flash) and Kodak Color Print Material Type C, is the successful combination that opened the door to color prints of fine quality. A wedding album of "natural Color" photographs has become a reality.

Kodacolor roll film is most versatile in that both daylight and clear flashbulb exposures can be made on the same roll without the need for filters. The advantages of such a simplification are obvious. Shooting a candid wedding with Kodacolor is as convenient as shooting with black and white: one film for both indoor and outdoor. And though Kodacolor's latitude approximates that of the transparency materials, it has an important difference: The result of Kodacolor is a color negative and correction of color balance is possible during the printing on color paper.

Kodacolor daylight film speed (index 32) is the same as for 35mm Ekta-chrome Daylight; clear flashbulb guide numbers are the same as for Ekta-chrome Type F, Other than the fact that one film takes care of all your

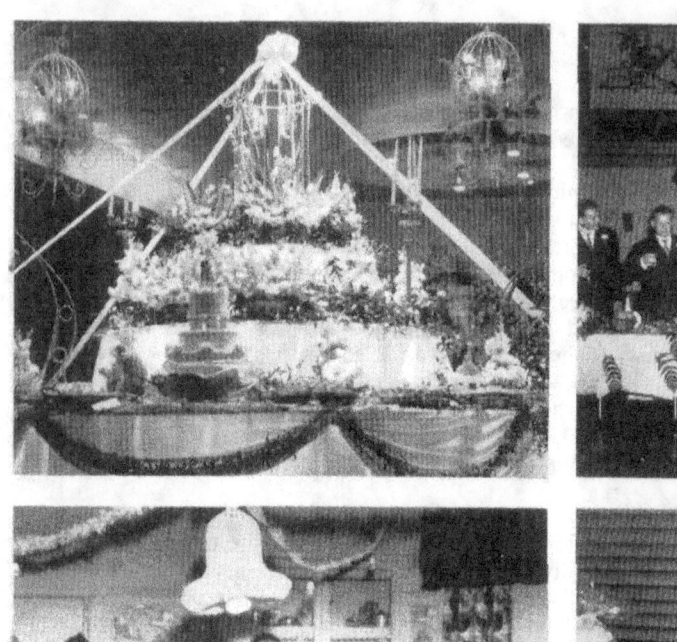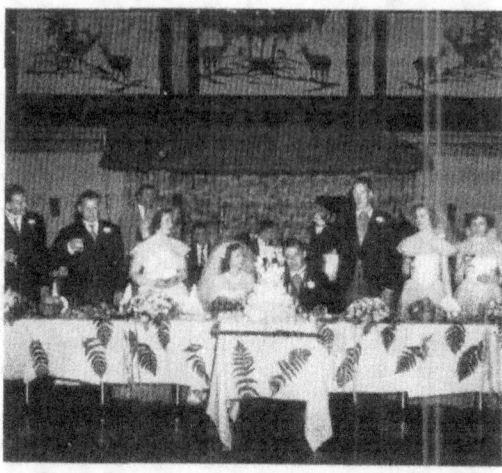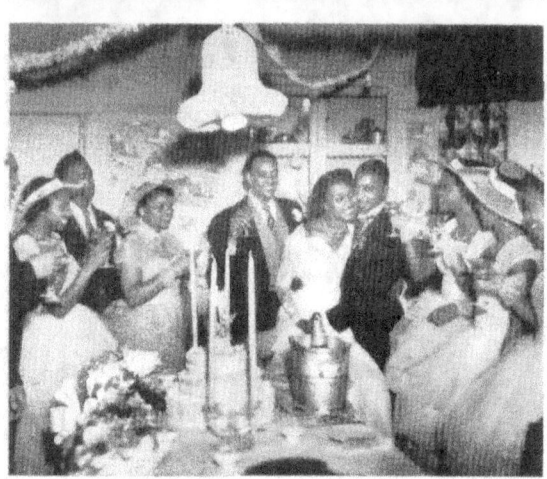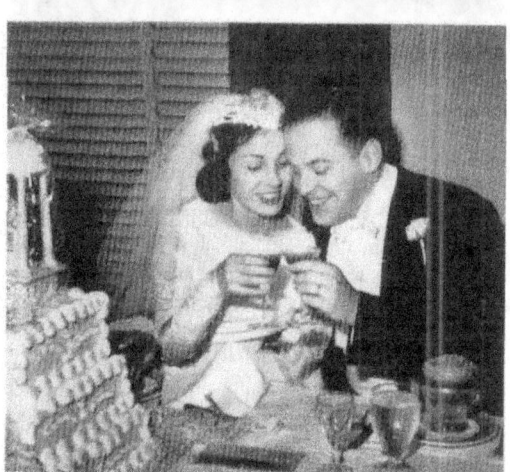

62. *The Smorgasbord is often a work of art. It pays to include it in the album. This one was shot with Rolleiflex, Tri-X, f/8, 4 seconds with camera on tripod.* 63, 64 *(upper right, lower left). When space permits, include the whole table as the party toasts the couple. If you must shoot from one end of the table, even out the light by focusing and setting the f/stop for the couple but aim the reflector at the farthest part of the table. The examples show both a formal and an informal arrangement of the party.* (63: Busch Pressman; Tri-X; No. 5 flashbulb, 1/50, f/11; DK-50. 64: Busch Pressman; Tri-X; 60 w/s electronic flash, 1/250, f/8; DK-50.) 65 *(lower right). The picture of the couple toasting each other should be taken from about 10 feet. You may include the best man and maid of honor if you choose. (Rolleiflex; Verichrome Pan; 80 w/s unit, 1/250 second, f/11; developed in D-76.)*

shooting, Kodacolor can be handled the same as Ektachrome. Processing laboratories have one suggestion: Try to avoid mixing daylight and tungsten light sources in the same shot. For instance, use a blue flashbulb for synchro-sunlight fill-in. A clear bulb fill-in would result in a color negative that might confuse the laboratory technician at the time of making a color print. Kodacolor can be processed by the photographer, by independent laboratories, or by Kodak. Ektacolor is not processed by Kodak.

Kodak Color Print Material Type C is a paper capable of making high-quality color enlargements from color negative material such as Kodacolor and Ektacolor negative film. In quality a Type C print may be likened to a Dye Transfer print. Though not so flexible as the Dye Transfer material, Type C paper permits considerable control of color contrast and of manipulation through dodging and burning-in. As with Kodacolor, Type C prints can be made by the photographer, a commercial laboratory, or by Kodak.

Owners of press-type cameras should use Kodak Ektacolor, Type S (for exposures of 1/25 second or faster) when they intend to make color prints or have them made. For best results and color negatives with reasonably uniform color balance Kodak advises exposing without a filter for clear flash shots; with Kodak Wratten Filter No. 85C for daylight; and with No. 85 for electronic flash. The Exposure Index for this film used in daylight with an 85C filter, is 25. Flashbulb guide numbers are the same as for roll film Kodacolor.

12.

Getting Started in Business

THE GOOD CANDID WEDDING photographer (often called the "following photographer" by the public) is partly born and partly made. The necessary ingredients are experience and the heart of an amateur. To start out, shoot a lot of flash: parties, babies, family groups—anything! You will be in luck if you can find an experienced candid man willing to have you shoot, along with him, on several of his weddings. Then do at least five or six weddings on your own for friends or relatives who do not wish to incur the expense of professional pictures. Do not mislead them as to your ability, and charge only for materials. Do not shoot for profit until you are absolutely sure you can produce results that approach professional standards. Nothing can compensate for wedding pictures that did not "turn out." Wedding photos are "for keeps." Develop your own negatives and do your own printing. This is the only satisfactory method for learning to judge the accuracy of your exposures and for learning to adjust the contrast of your film to suit your particular paper and enlarger.

The Weekend Candid Photographer

Your next logical step is to hang on to your regular job, whatever it is, and do candid weddings on weekends. Many photographers find this a source of welcome additional income, as well as an excellent transition step towards doing candid photography full-time.

Most of the business material in Chapter 13 will apply to you, as well as the man shooting candid weddings on a full-time basis.

People in small towns soon get to know the man shooting candid weddings on his weekends. Most of his work will come through recommendation. To the more enterprising, the extra labor of checking the local paper for engagement announcements will provide a list of leads, for contact by mail, telephone, or by dropping in with samples. If the quality of your work is good and the prices right, you will get your share of weddings.

In the larger town or in cities, the situation is not this simple. Every conceivable angle is exploited by the full-time studios. Bucking them would be an almost complete waste of time. Your work will have to come through recommendation and people you know who are getting married—and people are getting married all the time! Weddings in New York City (population about 8,000,000) are about 68,000 a year; in Newark, N.J., (population about 450,000), 5,000 a year; in Elizabeth, N.J. (population about 113,000), 1,200 a year.

Another Solution

For the photographer who does not care to sacrifice his weekends in shooting and his evenings in the darkroom processing and printing, shooting Saturdays and Sundays for studios is the answer. The general pay is $15 to $20 for a wedding, plus five to ten cents per shot for use of his electronic flash, and about five cents per mile car expense for the more distant weddings.

Candids are the life-blood of portrait studios; not many can exist without them. The busier the studio the greater their dependence on the free-lance candid wedding photographer. Visit their studios and show them a sample of your wedding work. If it is good, you will get plenty of calls. Good photographers are at a premium.

Going *into Business—The Next Step*

Now you have shot quite a few weekend weddings and you're feeling your photographic oats. In fact, you think you're good. Of late, somewhere in the back of your mind has been a vague but persistent notion about going into business for yourself. Candid wedding photography, of course!

Remember that inexperience and incompetence are prime causes of business failure. Some years ago I visited a friend at his place of business. The store—one of the larger in town—had been started by his father. Our conversation turned to the early and trying days of their business. What, I asked his father, did most to contribute to his success? He thought a moment. "The experience I gained from two previous business failures and the fact that I seldom make the same mistake twice."

This year about 13,000 business firms of all sorts will fail in this country. Their creators had the same high hopes and aspirations you have. Most of these failures will wipe out their owners and seriously affect their families. These are the cold hard facts. On the credit side of the picture is the 54 percent of businesses that will exist beyond the five-year period. And you have every right to think that yours will be one of these. There is only one way to find out!

A Practical Approach

To the not easily discouraged my advice is: Get a job with a local studio. If you can, choose one whose work you admire. Avoid one with many employees or you may find yourself stuck with one job for a long time, perhaps a rudimentary one of washing and drying prints. Avenues of learning will be limited and your progress slow.

A studio with one or two employees affords a greater opportunity for you to become a part of all its functions. Your duties will be varied. The average

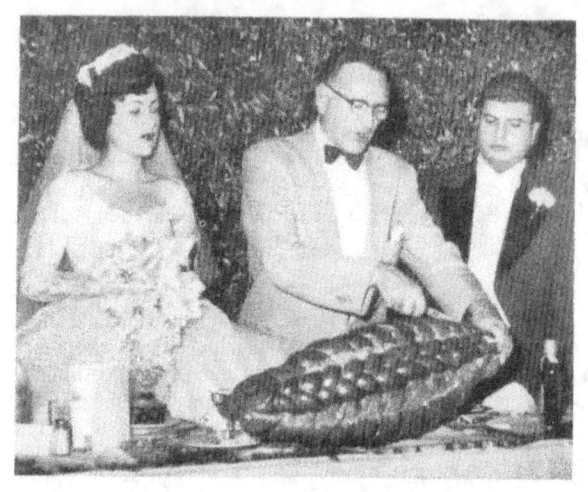

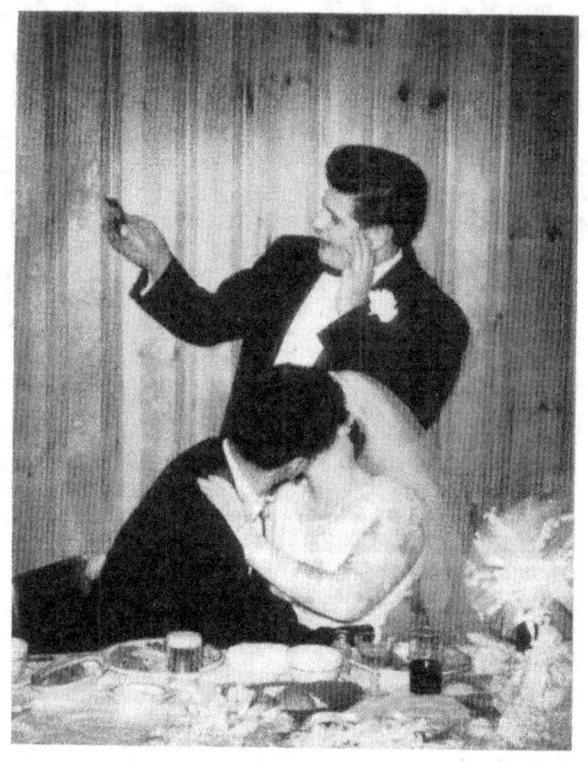

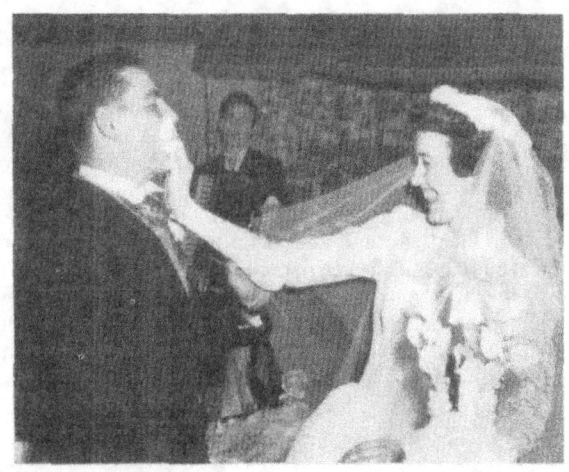

66. *The breaking of bread (opposite, top) is a ceremony which is customary at the beginning of the dinner following the Jewish wedding. It is one of the shots which you should get for the album. (Rolleifiex; Tri-X; 60 tv/s electronic flash unit, 1 1200 second, f/8; film developed in Microdol.)* 67. *Gag shots (opposite, lower) such as this one of the couple kissing while the best man or an usher holds a watch as if to time them, are included in the coverage of many weddings. Always remember that the shots you take are intended for their album and should reflect their taste. (Retina 11a; Plm-X; No. 5 bulb, 1/200, f/11; developed in Microdol.)* 68. *The wedding coverage should include a shot of the bride feeding wedding cake to the groom, the groom feeding cake to the bride or a picture of them feeding each other. The picture above is unusual in the vigor with which the bride is feeding the groom. You should always be alert for these unexpected happenings. (Busch Pressman; Tri-X; 80 w/s electronic flash, 1/200, f/16; DK-50.)*

studio handles child and adult portraiture, wedding photography and commercial work. You will develop negatives, see how negatives are retouched, make prints and do print finishing. Part of your work may even include the important business end of ordering supplies, selling and bookkeeping. You will learn how a studio is operated—by doing just that!

In the meantime you can put what you have learned into practice by taking on wedding jobs in your spare time. Of course this work on your own time *must not in any way* conflict with the studio's business. At the same time gather all the business facts you can. For advice talk to your local Chamber of Commerce and to your bank. Write to Eastman Kodak Co., Ansco, DuPont and the Department of Commerce in Washington, D.C.

The Final Step

When will you be ready to go on your own? You'll know. I'd say about the time you *think* you can do everything as well as your employer—or maybe better. Tread cautiously. Think back to the days before you had this practical studio experience. You've learned a lot since. You have a lot more to learn!

Your next step? That depends on the size of your ambition and the amount of money you have. Several months rent as security usually is required by most landlords for desirable locations. Unless you are handy with tools and can do much of the work yourself, I would say you need a minimum of two to four thousand dollars for a presentable studio if no major alterations (such as rebuilding window fronts) are contemplated. There is plumbing, electrical work, painting, partitions, and purchase of drapes, rugs, studio furniture, files, sinks, to mention only the obvious. Photographic equipment, of course, is extra.

After you have figured all your studio costs, add what you will need to support yourself and your dependents for a minimum of six months. Your business may not be self-supporting for this long a period—maybe longer.

Your studio doors are open. Now you will have to do everything your former employer did and maybe more. (See Chapter 13 on Business.) Every month or so you will have to change the pictures in your window or display case. You will have to explore the possibilities of advertising: newspaper, magazine, direct mail, handbills, billboard, and in smaller towns where the cost is not prohibitive, radio. There is no set pattern. A medium of advertising that does well in one locality may be ineffective in another. Your local Chamber of Commerce should be able to advise which mediums have proved the most effective in your community.

An alternative to the higher rent downstairs studio is an upstairs location, preferably with a display space on the ground floor. For the man whose funds are limited but whose determination is not, a happy compromise is a house that can serve as studio and residence.

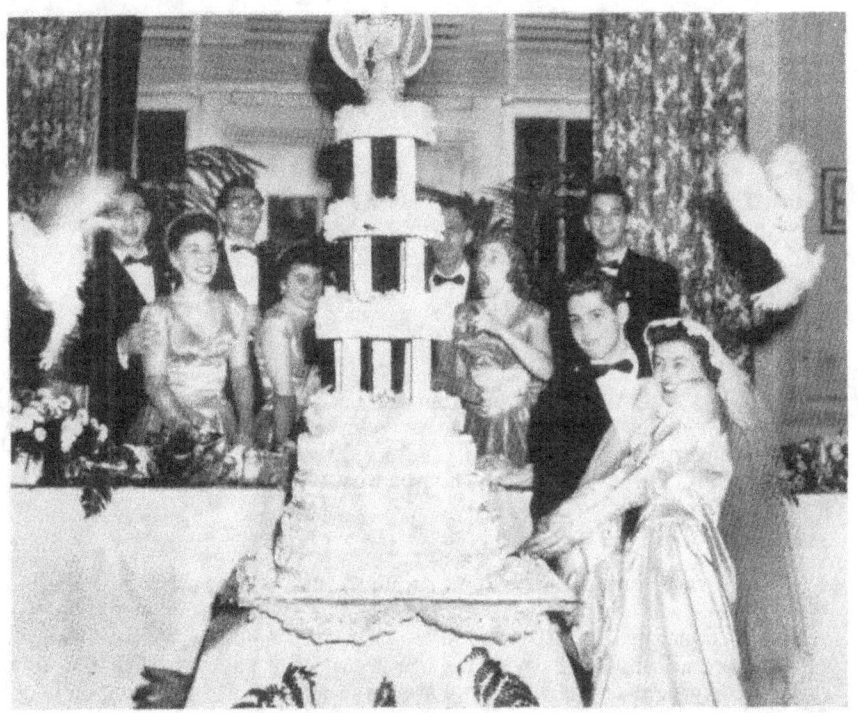

69. *The cake cutting shot is important. However, one with this much animation is the exception. Usually the couple is placed so that the wall behind the bridal table is the background. Shoot from about 10 feet. Detail in the cake and modeling on the couple will be improved by raising the gun high over your head. Do not hold the flash gun to the left or right as this may produce bad shadows from one or another of the subjects or from the cake itself. Try to separate the couple's hands from the cake so the latter may be burned in during printing without blackening the hands. For the photograph above 1 had been tipped off that the pigeons would be released so I stood about 20 to 25 feet back from the cake. (In printing, the non-essentials have been cropped out.) I used a No. 5 flashbulb because electronic flash would have frozen the movement of the birds and produced a static result. The camera was a Busch Pressman; the film, Tri-X developed in DK-50. The shutter setting was 1/100 second at f/5.6.*

13.

Business Procedures

SELLING is ABOUT THE MOST important part of your business both before and after you shoot the wedding. Whatever your method of making the original contact—advertising, telephone solicitation, direct mail, or other—it will turn out a total loss if you can't get the couple to say yes, and to leave a deposit.

Salesmanship Before the Wedding

The person showing the sample albums is the hub of all your operations —the person who gets that "Yes, we'd like you to shoot our wedding." Not everyone is qualified to sell. A likeable personality, sincerity, and knowing the business are all important. With the turning of each page there should be an easy, running commentary that points out the quality of the photographs, the detail in the gown or cake, the effective draping of the gown, the realistic third dimensional effect of available light, the grouping of the bridal party, the beauty of a synchro-sunlight portrait, etcetera, etcetera, etcetera.

If the couple you are seeing are friends or relatives of someone whose wedding pictures you have done—and done well—you will have very little selling left to do. On the other hand, if your contact is in response to one of your advertisements or solicitations, selling will not be easy. Your work will have to sell *itself,* you will have to sell *yourself* and the prices will have to sell *themselves.* At first everything you say will be open to suspicion—you are trying to get their business. But the longer you can keep them interested, the friendlier they will get. If you are sincere, little by little their suspicions will disappear. This often takes an hour or more.

What do you say to them? Nothing and everything. Be enthusiastic about your photography. Know your competition and be honest in your replies to their questions. You will need no prepared talk, the right words will come out.

Sample Albums

Your sample candid wedding albums are your most important salesmen. Silent though they are, they can say enough to make or break your sale. The

116

average prospective bride and groom may not know much about the technicalities of photography but they have been conditioned by the ever present advertising photograph to sense a good picture. If your work has not impressed them they are not apt to tell you so. Instead, they will put you off by saying they would like to think it over.

There are two ways of putting together a sample book. One is to include about thirty pictures showing the same bride in the sequence in which they were taken. There is a reason for stopping at this number instead of including more of your work. Often the couple will ask the price of an album the size of the sample. Most couples have a vague idea of the cost of candid wedding coverage, and a price of $150 or more for a book of fifty pictures may frighten them away. It is true that after trying one or two more studios they will realize that your prices are competitive and that wedding albums are not inexpensive. But this is little consolation, once the other studio has signed them.

The other way to compile a sample book is to use a different bride (and groom) for every picture. This will increase the possibility of your customer's recognizing one of the bridal couples. Up to now they have been judging your work with caution. They know it is your best. But, if "Mary's" or "John's" pictures "turned out" well enough to be used as samples. . . . You should have a different album for each of the three major faiths: Catholic, Protestant, Jewish.

3D, on the other hand, is no problem as the transparencies are individual. The couple will usually start with your basic price (see below). Most couples will not be too concerned with the cost of the extra slides until they are ready to order. If your work is good, the temptation will be too great for them to resist buying more pictures. They will rationalize their photographic expenditures with, "You only get married once!"

Appointment Books

The following is the format I use in entering an appointment in my books. (One is my personal pocket size loose-leaf notebook; the other is an appointment book for the office.)

Date of wedding   Time of ceremony
Black & White   3D   35mm slides   8x10 color prints
Bride's last name)
) First names as they will appear on album cover
Groom's last name) Bride's home address and telephone Where bride is dressing—at home, or elsewhere Church: address, denomination, and time (double check time) Distance from bride's house to church
Place of reception, address, telephone (so photographer can be reached)
Time of reception
Number in bridal party   Deposit: cash or check

This same information is repeated in the office appointment book on the page of the wedding date.

When the couple order on their proofs, a card is filed with the same information but under the groom's last name, and including their new address

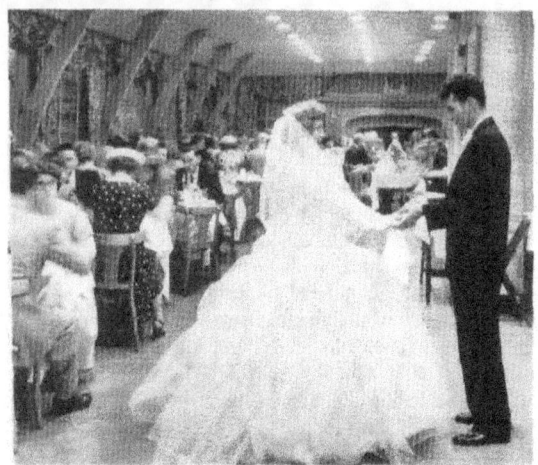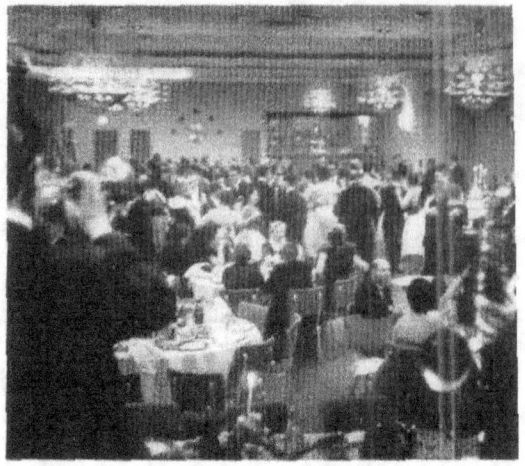

70, 71. An *over-all photograph of fairly large reception halls cannot be taken from the floor with a single flashbulb. It may he done, however, from an elevation such as a balcony or stairway. Extension cords for supplementary flash are an invitation to an accident and slave units are usually impossible under these circumstances. Available light is frequently the answer. It is best to wait until the guests are seated for dinner so movement will be at a minimum. These pictures show two solutions to this problem. The one left was made with a Rolleiflex with Tri-X film and the couple posed for a 6-second exposure at f/11. The picture right was made with a Nikon using the 35mm Nikkor lens and Tri-X film exposed at 1/30 second and f/8 and developed in FR X-500 (diluted 1:10). If you cover with sheet film you might take along one or two holders with Royal-X Pan film to cope with situations such as this.*

and telephone number. Negatives can be filed under the groom's name in alphabetical order. I use a 5x7 envelope with a flap to keep the dust out. A shoe box makes a good file.

Promotion

Promotion, photographically speaking, is the art of getting people to buy more than they had originally intended. It is selling the icing on the cake. Promotion is a vital yet sensitive part of the photography business. It is *vital,* particularly to studios, for the additional revenue it provides can mean the difference between profit and loss. It is *sensitive,* in that it must be treated with a light hand; pressed too hard it can frighten business away. It calls for intuition and the power of suggestion. The salesperson skilled in promotion never feels it necessary to apply the discomforting tactics of high pressure. He *suggests.* With subtlety and imagination he endows the item he is selling with more value and desirability than the money it costs. And after the wedding the customer ends by believing that everything ordered was his wish—and necessary to his happiness. This type of promotion can be likened to radio's and television's "soft sell." We are being sold and we like it!

Here are some of the extras or "icing" that can be suggested by the candid wedding photographer when the couple is ordering.

Black and white: A musical album instead of the standard type; small albums for the parents; coloring of photos; wallet size photos or "Thank you" cards; an 8x10 copy of their wedding announcement for the first page of the album; 11x14 or larger prints of their candid wedding portraits, possibly colored; frames.

Color: Color enlargements from 35mm or stereo transparencies; an electrically powered viewer instead of the battery one.

With either black-and-white or color coverage of the wedding, an after-the-wedding studio sitting of the bride may be suggested. The gown, other than needing a pressing, usually is in good condition. Even if the train or hem is soiled, it should be no deterrent as the most popular composition for a bridal portrait, is three-quarter length.

The after-the-wedding studio sitting may serve as the basis for a "heavy oils" portrait. Heavy oils are used to opaque the background and accentuate the hair, eyes, lips, gown, veil, flowers, etc., to simulate an artist's painting of a portrait. Prices are more expensive than those charged for tints, and can best be determined by comparing those current with your local studios.

Stereo

A good promotional item is a case that holds the stereo slides and viewer. It is made with a white cover and gold leaf lettering, to simulate a wedding album. The interior has compartments and is in velvet or attractive materials. Suggest color enlargements from single stereo frames. Suggest a duplicate set of stereos with viewer for the parents.

My practice has been to have my 3D stereos mounted. They are shown in the cardboard mount and only the ones selected by the couple are put in frames. It is more than worth the difference in processing costs.

When the stereos are being selected, a great deal of time may be saved by projecting a single frame in a 35mm projector instead of looking at them in the viewer. You can control the time of each frame's projection, whereas with the viewer, it is held as long as each person wishes to hold it! It is the first time they are seeing them—and they are reluctant to let them go. And where more than the couple are present, this may run into hours of time. Before projecting the rest of the candid wedding, let the couple see their formals in the 3D viewer. This will satisfy their desire to see what the stereo is like.

How to *Charge for Your Pictures*

One way to charge is for each picture, with a 20- to 24-picture album minimum. A general price is $3 for each photo whether it is in the book or in a folder.

Another method is a package deal. A competitive price is in the neighborhood of $75 or $85 and consists of:

20 photos including the album and gold leaf lettering 1 11x14
tinted photograph of the bride, or bride and groom 10 or 12
"Thank You" photo cards.

Each additional photo is about $3 whether it is in the book or in a folder. The general practice is to submit either a black and white or sunproof of each negative. Through these the couple can select the pictures for their album and also the ones they will give as gifts. "Thank-you" cards are on deckle-edge paper, usually $4^1/4$x$5^1/2$ inches, or a wallet size folder with a picture of the couple and a "Thank You" message. With the folder type, a wallet-size photo is inserted; with the deckle-edge type, a mask that your dealer can supply, is needed.

Frequently individual members of the bridal party ask you to take pictures of themselves. What should you charge them for prints? Charge the same price the bridal couple is paying for their extras (about $3) but add a dollar to the price of the first photo to cover the cost of postage, handling, and a photo-mailer.

Type of Albums

The album used by most studios is of the "slip-in" type. The photographs are easily slipped into the album leaves and are protected by a sheet of acetate. The cover is of a washable (composition) material. "Our Wedding Day" is on the cover in gold leaf. The bride's and groom's first names and their wedding date is added to the cover when the album is ordered. All camera shops carry one or more of this style album. A second type with a genuine leather cover, comes in several colors. Ivory is appropriate and very popular. It can be purchased in both the slip-in and dry-mount type leaf. The leather album is about twice the price of the washable album.

Suggest small albums for the parents. An average price, including a good quality small album is: twelve photos for $20 and $1.50 for each additional print. The usual size of these photos is 4x5.

For Stereo (3D Color)

An average price is $75 to $80 for 20 stereo slides with viewer; $3 for each additional slide. Stereo pairs should be bound in a metal or plastic binder and the film should be protected by plastic or glass.

When you are taking 3D formals, also take similar pictures in black and white. These pictures should be made of the bride, bride and groom, bridal party, and of the parents with the couple so that prints can be ordered for gifts. The extra black-and-white photos will add substantially to the size of the total order. The couple can be informed that, with the use of a Stereo-Daptor (or a similar unit), stereo slides can be viewed—though not in 3D— using many 35mm projectors that do not have this accommodation built in.

Color Prints—A Cost Item!

Kodacolor and Type C paper can produce fine prints, but the day has not arrived when the average photographer can go into his darkroom and "knock-off" a color print. It's not that easy. In fact, it's quite hard for even an ex-

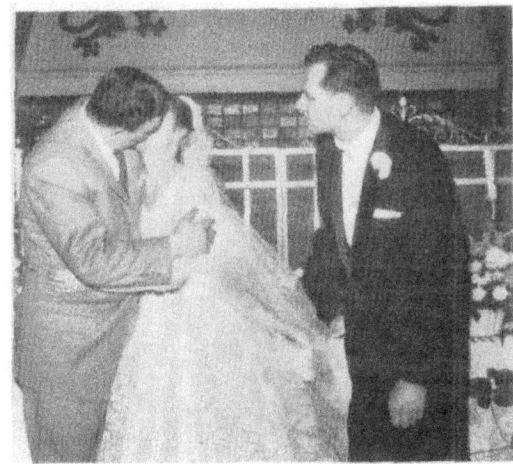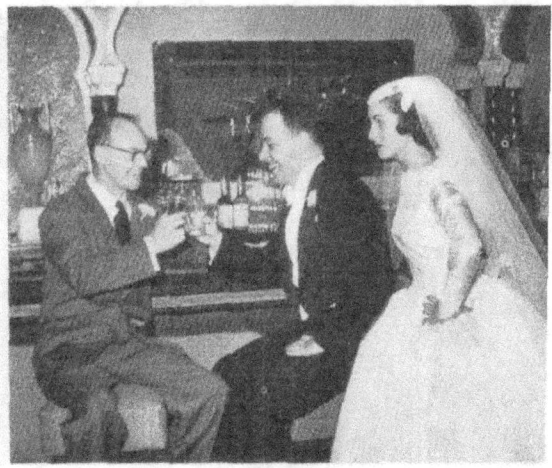

72, 73. *Here are two other "gag shots" which are frequently included in albums. In photo at left the groom is posed watching the bride being kissed by a friend. In picture at right the bride watches disapprovingly as the groom drinks with a member of the party. The success of pictures such as these will depend on how much the couple wants to "ham" for the camera. (72: Konica III; Plus-X; 80 w/s unit, 1/200, f/8. 73: Rolleiflex; Tri-X; 60 w/s unit, 1/250 second, f/8; films developed in Microdol.)*

perienced candid wedding photographer to make a good color print. Though he may be equipped to do it, the process involves numerous steps and considerable time.

The film is here, the paper is here, but why has it not caught on like wildfire, as has 3D stereo color? For one thing, color print making as we have said, is not simple enough for most photographers to handle. And it is time consuming. For another, having prints made by commercial laboratories, though reasonable for an occasional print, adds up to a lot of money for an album of 30 or more photographs. Let us break down the costs of producing a candid wedding in 8x10 color prints.

These are Kodak's prices on cost of film and processing.

Kodacolor Firm, cost of 4 No. 120 rolls @ $1 per roll	$ 4.00
Flashbulbs	4.25
Processing of film @ $.90 per roll	3.60
Set of 48 2Y4X2V4 color proofs @ $.32 per print	15.36
Cost of 30 8x10 Type C prints @ $3.50 per print (This is the rub)	105.00
Album for 30 photographs	13.00
Gold leaf lettering	1.00
Total (Approximate)	$146.21

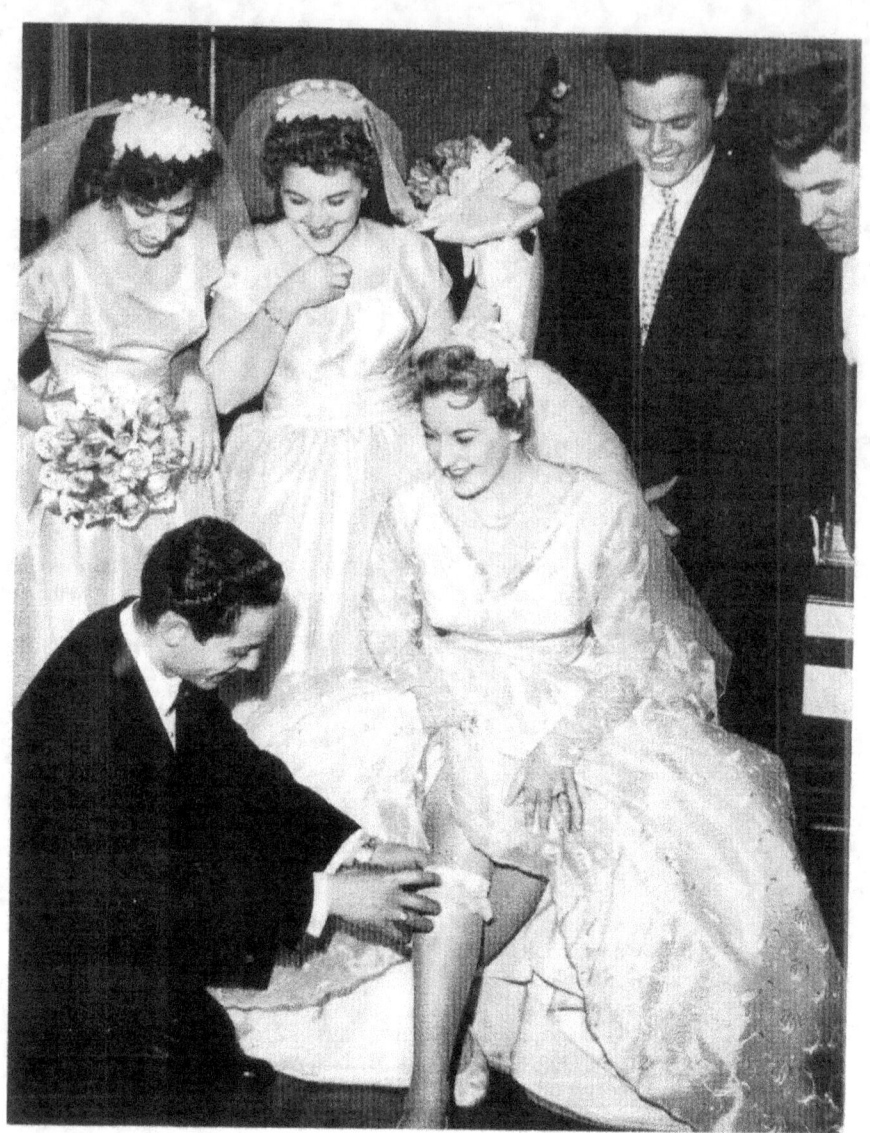

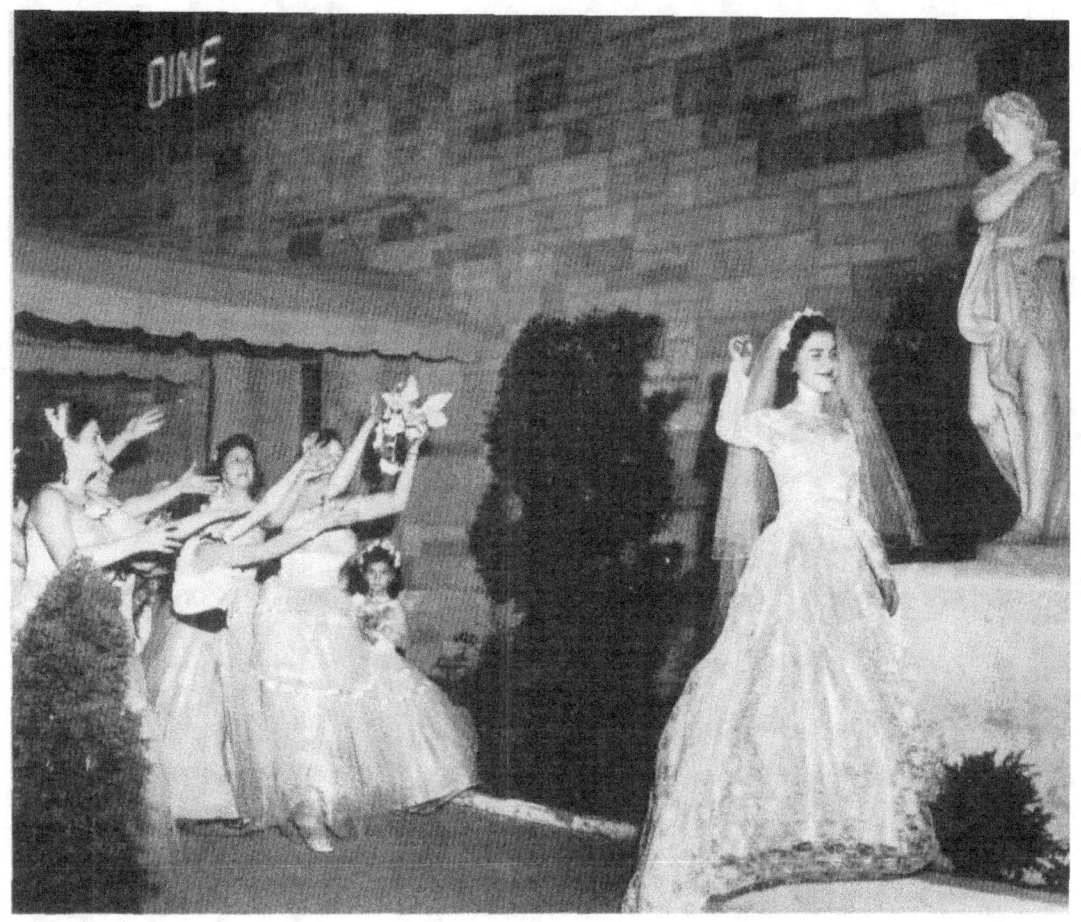

74 *(opposite). One customary incident at many weddings is for the bride to throw her garter to the boys in the audience. This photo shows the groom removing the garter just before it is tossed. The gown should not be raised above the knee lest the picture cease to be amusing and become bad taste. The other people in the group should all be looking in the same direction, either at the garter itself or at the couple. I usually stage this shot sometime before the garter is actually thrown in order to secure it without being hurried. (Rolleiflex; Tri-X; 60 w/s electronic flash, 1/250, f/8; developed in Microdol.)*
75 *(above). A key photo is the one of the bride throwing her bouquet to the girls in the wedding party. The bride should stand on an elevation, frequently the stairs. She should, turn her back to the girls (as tradition dictates) and at the count of three throw her flowers and quickly turn to face the group. The girls should be about 15 to 20 feet from the bride. The picture may be made either on a line with the group of girls or at one side of the bride next to her throwing arm. Do not be in a hurry to shoot, but wait until the bouquet has nearly reached the group when there will be the greatest animation. In the shot of the bride throwing the garter she can be in the same spot with the boys where the girls stood. (Busch Pressman; Tri-X; 80 w/s electronic flash unit, 1/200 second, f/8; developed in DK-50.)*

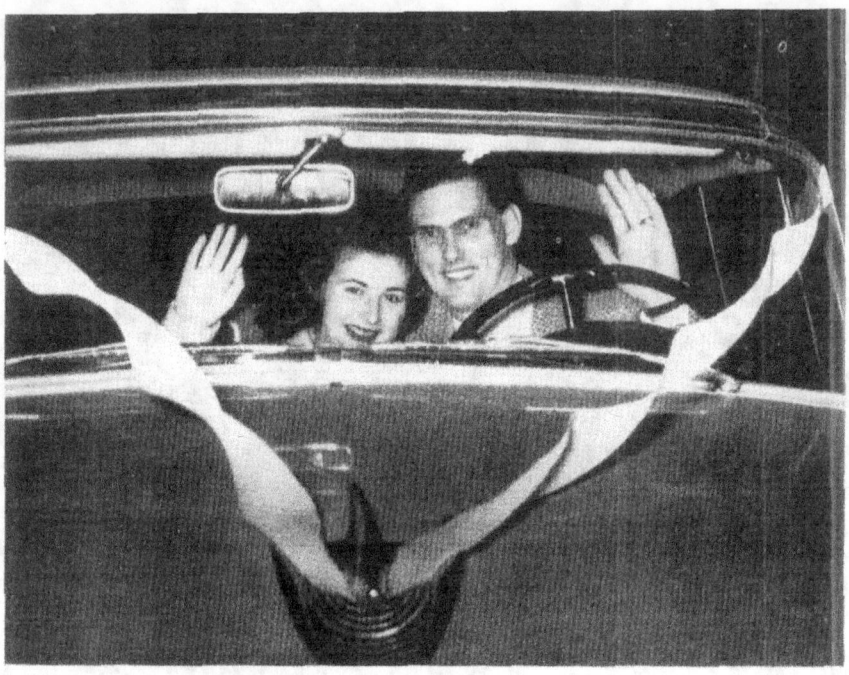

76. *Waving good-bye from the car makes another interesting -final picture. Shoot from about 12 to 15 feet and be sure that the faces are not obstructed by windshield wiper, rear view mirror or window post. (Rolleiflex; Tri-X; 80 w/s electronic flash unit:, 1/250 second, f/9; developed in MicrodoL)*

In the New York area prices now average about $250 for an album with 24 color prints. The ordinary couples that make up the buying public, and provide the major part of our business, can't afford these prices! It might pay the candid wedding photographer to price the independent laboratories as many are offering special discounts to attract the photographic trade. But no matter what the discount, the cost to the photographer is still heavy.

But why not suggest one roll in color of the formals (they are especially beautiful when taken outdoors) and a shot or two in church? The balcony and floor shots are very dramatic in color. The color photographs, in their proper sequence, can be added to the black-and-white album, or be placed in folders, to be given as gifts.

Duplicate the color photos in black and white until you know what you are doing. For a start, why not shoot an occasional roll on speculation? *But* familiarize yourself with this type of color so that if that day arrives when your favorite photo mag's headlines shout "Costs no more than black and white; Color prints in a minute; Do it yourself." You will be ready. We can dream, can't we?

Method of Payments

Different locations, different clientele, require individual handling. But you will never find yourself getting into trouble if you keep your candid wedding business strictly on a cash and carry basis. Following is the method of payment practiced by most studios:

77. This -picture is posed to suggest the couple stealing away. An alternative is to have them embrace cheek-to-cheek and wave good-bye. You may end the album with a picture such as this. (Minolta Autocord; Tri-X; 80 w/s unit, 1/200, f/11.)

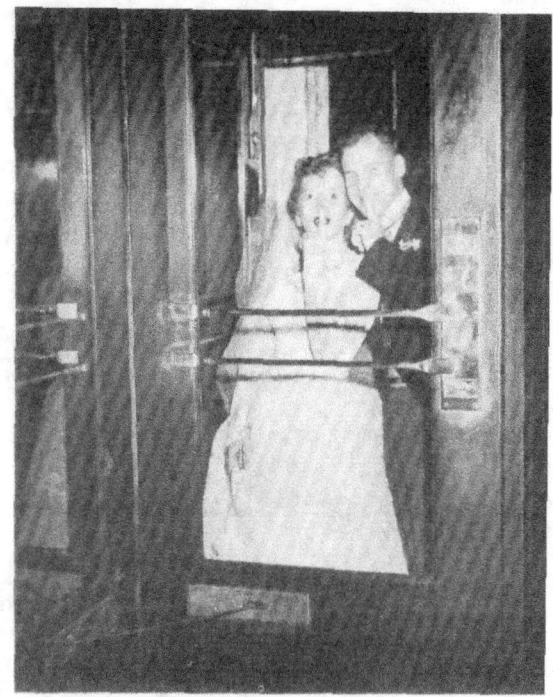

1. A substantial deposit ($25.00 or more) when the wedding is booked.
2. When the pictures are ordered, one half of the remaining balance.
3. The final balance when the work is picked up.

With this method the payments are stretched over a period of several months. The payments are easier for the couple and at the same time the studio is covering its expense by working with the couple's money.

Bookkeeping

Compared to most retail businesses the daily transactions of a photographic studio are few. Also, not many items are necessary for its operation and about half a dozen suppliers can fill your needs. Bookkeeping for a studio is simple,

Your books are the barometer of your business. They let you know how it is faring and can foretell weaknesses in its structure. At any time you can see how you stand. Simple though they may be, they must be accurate. A man new in business is wise to retain an accountant to set up a bookkeeping system and to have him check the books periodically. At the end of the year he can attend to your income tax reports and by taking advantage of every allowance to which your business is legally entitled, possibly save you money. His business is business and his advice can be invaluable. The cost of his services is reasonable. With time you will become familiar with his system and might decide to keep your own books.

What Does a Candid Wedding Cost You?

Now that you know what to charge for a candid wedding, what does each one cost you in terms of materials, processing, albums, etc.? Here is the ap-

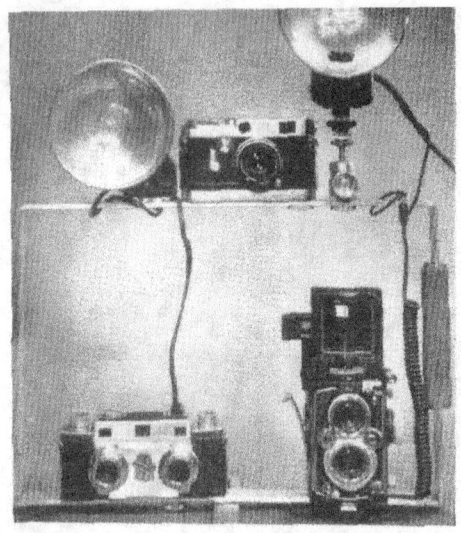
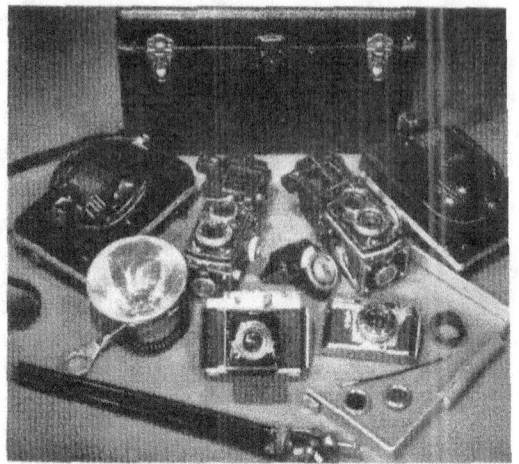

proximate breakdown for two types of candid weddings: The black-and-white wedding, and the 3D Color (Stereo) Candid. Listed only are direct shooting costs. Overhead and similar items have been eliminated as they vary greatly. If you're a free-lance who shoots only on weekends and has no studio, they will be negligible. Also eliminated are the extra black-and-white shots you'll take when covering a 3D Candid.

Cost of Producing a Black-and-White Candid (approximate)

1. Film (4x5 sheet film)	$ 6.50
2. Flashbulbs	5.50
3. Developer (for film)	.60
4. Proofs (paper)	.60
5. Developer (for proofs and prints)	.25
6. Paper (8x10) for book of 30 pictures, allowing an sheet for every four prints.	extra 3.00
7. Paper for 10 extra prints in folders, allowing an sheet for every four prints.	extra .90
8. Alburn: washable type with leaves for thirty prints.	13.00
9. Gold-leaf lettering of couple's names	1.00
10. Folders for extra prints (10)	1.60
Total	$32.95

Where electronic flash, film pack or roll film are used in place of the above items, an adjustment in costs must be made. The above is a cost of materials alone, and does not include such expenses as car, depreciation of equipment, rent, telephone, advertising, stamps, etc. For the man who shoots an occasional candid wedding and whose darkroom is at home, the addition of about three dollars should cover his gasoline, stationery and postal charges.

Approximate Cost of Producing a Candid in 3D Color (Stereo)

1. Film, 56 exp. 2 rolls (28 exp. to a 35 exp. roll)	$5.20
2. Film (2 rolls) Processed & stereo mounted (Kodak's price)	7.00
3. Flashbulbs	5.00
4. Frames	3.50
5. Viewer	12.75
Total	$33.45

78 (left). I designed this bracket to hold several cameras. The inside dimen sions are 11% inches by 16% inches and the material is 1x3/16-inch alumi num strip which is available in many hardware stores. Quarter-inch holes with 20 threads per inch were tapped in three sides of the frame to hold cameras and lights. The piece at right angles on the bottom acts as a stand. The electronic flash reflector is on a tilt-top head and adjusts for bounce light.
79 (right). This is my equipment for wedding coverage: a case; Matador 1 electronic flash; Rolleiflex with Rolleimeter; GE Guardian meter with Dyna-Cell; another Rollei; a Mamiya 6 and Konica III; a tripod, cable release, lens shade and 10X neutral density and yellow filters. The bracket is 11% inches high with 5%-inch and 7%-inch arms. It will take one or two cameras and a flash unit.

Conclusion

TIME WAS when a candid photographer's life was simple. It was a case of, "You pays yer money and you takes yer choice." "Yer choice," could mean only Ansco or Kodak. Mostly it was Kodak's Super XX or Super Panchro Press Type B, and for flash a No. 5 or 25 bulb.

Today life is not so simple. "You pays yer money" and you ask for super-fast Tri-X.

"But," whispers your dealer, reaching under the counter, "haven't you heard of Ilford HPS?—twice as fast as Tri-X!"

A week later you walk in. Proudly you lay your pictorial efforts on his counter. "Yup," he says dismissing them with a dutiful glance, "that Ilford is good, but friend have I got dynamite! Just try this one! . . ." And so it goes. Photographers go about their work with an air of nervous preoccupation. They are insecure. Any day now someone will announce that the new, miracle film they've succeeded in mastering is now a "has been."

The story does not end here. There are the new, high-energy Phenidone developers, Ilford's Microphen and FR's X-500, for example. The M2 flashbulb is hardly hatched before it's being improved and crowding the also new No. 8 out of the picture. No. 5, referred to as "midget" feels huge and clumsy when placed beside the "peanut-size" breed. *And so it goes. . . .*

Well, I believe I've covered all that needs saying here, but if there be truth in the Chinese proverb, "one picture is worth a thousand words," the rest can be said best by the pictures themselves. So less of words and let the photos do the talking. Now follow me while I shoot a wedding.

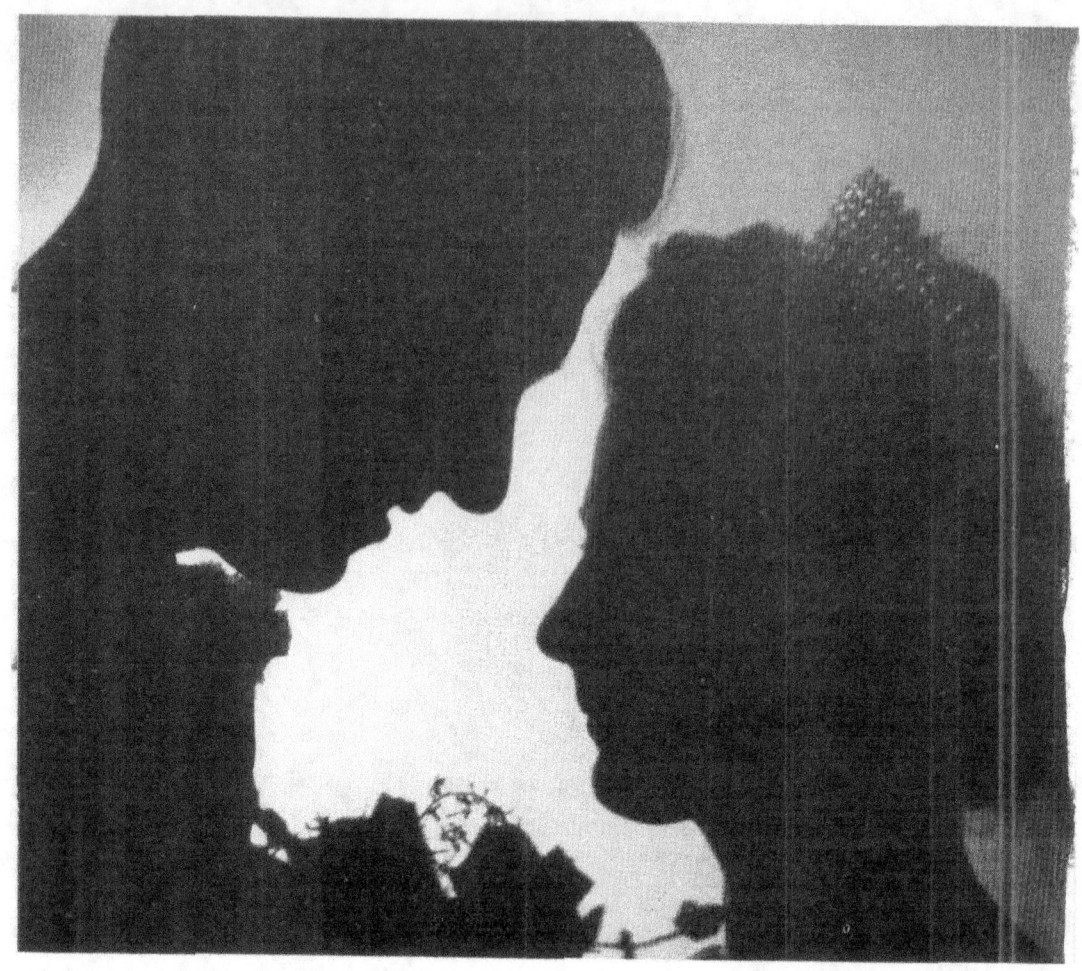

80. *These young faces with their attractive profiles invited this approach. A silhouette was created with the light of a table lamp behind the couple. Tri-X film was exposed in the Rolleiflex at 1/30 and f/3.5 and developed in Microdol. Another way to make a silhouette is to point an extension flash at the wall from behind the couple. Use the same shutter speed that you would with direct flash.*

Also available from:
www.sunvillagepublications.com

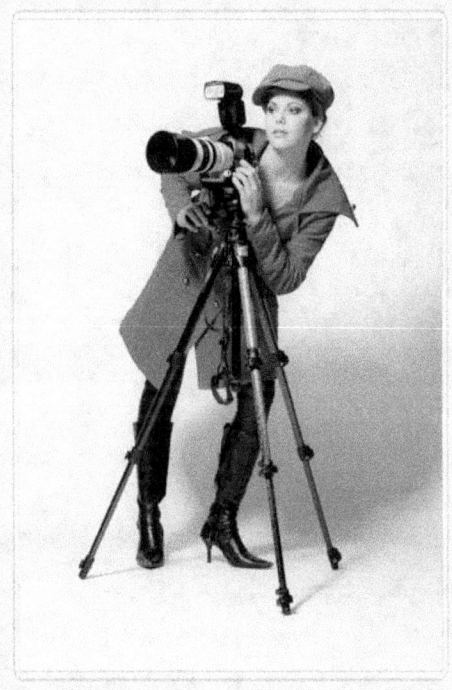

Posing For The Camera

a professional guide for the creative model, director and photographer

Harriett Shepard & Lenore Meyer

www.ingramcontent.com/pod-product-compliance
Lightning Source LLC
Chambersburg PA
CBHW052000280526
45793CB00005B/794